SPARK!

SPARK!

QUICK WRITES TO KINDLE HEARTS AND MINDS IN ELEMENTARY CLASSROOMS

Paula Bourque

STENHOUSE PUBLISHERS
PORTSMOUTH, NEW HAMPSHIRE

www.stenhouse.com

Library of Congress Cataloging-in-Publication Data

Names: Bourque, Paula, 1963- author.
Title: Spark! : Quick writes to kindle hearts and minds in elementary classrooms /
    Paula Bourque.
Description: Portland, Maine : Stenhouse Publishers, [2019] | Includes
    bibliographical references.
Identifiers: LCCN 2018027708 (print) | LCCN 2018043323 (ebook) | ISBN
    9781625312013 (ebook) | ISBN 9781625312006 (pbk. : alk. paper)
Subjects: LCSH: English language—Composition and exercises—Study and
    teaching (Elementary) | Language arts (Elementary)
Classification: LCC LB1576 (ebook) | LCC LB1576 .B5328 2019 (print) | DDC
    372.62/3—dc23
LC record available at https://lccn.loc.gov/2018027708

Book design by Blue Design (www.bluedes.com)

Manufactured in the United States of America

PRINTED ON 30% PCW
RECYCLED PAPER

25 24 23 22 21 20 19   9 8 7 6 5 4 3 2 1

It's with a grateful heart that I dedicate this book to two strong women who have lifted me through this journey: Linda Rief, for her professional influence, and Kim Yaris, for her personal inspiration.

Here's to strong women. May we know them.

May we be them. May we raise them.

CONTENTS

Acknowledgments

Alone we can do so little; together
we can do so much.
—Helen Keller

No book ever comes together by the solitary efforts of an author. There are so many who have inspired, collaborated with, and mentored me through this process that I know I'm at risk of forgetting some.

Thank you to the fantastic teachers and students of the Augusta School Department: Jessica West, Karen Erdmann, Brandi Grady, Meg Dyer, Kaitie King, Janet Frake, Caroline Eldridge, Samantha Simmons, Erin Whitish, Andrea Bretschneider, Dan Johnston, Guy Meader, Maureen Cooper, Meagan Mattice, Jenna Sementelli, Samantha Esancy, Liz Chadwick, Becky Foster, Jessica Walling, Marcia Hughes, and Jessica Dejongh. You are a literacy coach's dream team!

Thank you to my Teach Write Tribe. Led by the amazing Jennifer Laffin, she and Andy Schoenborn, Michelle Haseltine, Jennifer Chafin, Krista Senatore, Jill Davidson, and Liz Garden read through my manuscript with the keen eyes of talented teacher writers. I wish all teachers had a support group like this to motivate and move their practice.

I am grateful to the entire Stenhouse team who are there for me with every step of my writing journey. My dream editor, Maureen Barbieri, continually inspires me with her knowledge of writing and her astute insights. She is a true mentor and friend I cannot begin to thank enough. I am forever grateful to Dan Tobin for recognizing the work of classroom teachers and publishing books that honor their passion and expertise. I am beholden to the behind-the-scenes help of Louisa Irele, Chandra Lowe, Jay Kilburn, Grace Makley, Chuck Lerch, Tom Morgan, Fay LaCasse, Jacqui Carr, Lynne Costa, and everyone else at Stenhouse for bringing this book to life.

My deepest thanks go to my loving family. My husband, Jim, is my rock. He makes this crazy life manageable with his love, patience, and encouragement. My kids, Bailey and Casey, motivate me to do and be my best. They have opened my heart and my eyes to the wonders of childhood, making me a better teacher, mother, and human being. I am humbled and blessed.

Introduction

We write for so many reasons, from practical to poetical. I want my students to embrace writing as a way of being human. Sadly, too many never fully realize the potential writing can bring to their lives. These children need a spark to ignite that passion, creativity, and awareness. My hope is that this book will provide those sparks and kindle a whole new appreciation not only for writing but also for the world within and around them.

I also know that time is a precious commodity in schools, so we need to spend it doing stuff that matters. Kindling our students' hearts and minds doesn't require excessive amounts of time, but it does require intention. I never want to do, or ask teachers to do, stuff that doesn't matter. We just don't have that luxury of time. For me, quick writing has been an effective and fun way of doing stuff that matters.

Volume Matters

Quantity produces quality. If you only write a few things, you're doomed.
—Ray Bradbury

If we want our students to become proficient writers we need to increase the amount of writing being expected and produced by our students. *Every. Single. Day.* Ask athletes, musicians, or artists how they excel at their craft, and they will all tell you the same thing: practice, practice, practice. We know this to be true, and yet we often have students who do a minimum amount of writing in our classrooms, especially our striving students who may be pulled out for services, whose language skills limit their output, or who spend more time *thinking* about what to write than actually putting those thoughts on paper. We need to carve out bits of time and take advantage of *writeable moments* in our classrooms each day to build up the volume that will move and improve our writers.

> I write to discover what I know.
> **—Flannery O'Connor**

Purpose Matters

Students need opportunities to write across the curriculum, not just in language arts, so they know what it's like to think as scientists, artists, mathematicians, and so on. They need opportunities to write beyond the curriculum to think like humans. If we compartmentalize writing into months-long genre studies, our students still need consistent practice with the other modes of writing during this time. Cycling through other genres with quick writes can keep those skills fresh and accessible. Writing isn't just a subject; it's a life skill. We always want our students to understand its purpose to be fully engaged.

> Writing, to me, is simply thinking through my fingers.
> **—Isaac Asimov**

Thinking Matters

Learning is more than retaining and recalling the *what* of our teaching; it is also interpreting and contemplating the *so what* of that information. It is not just remembering, it is thinking; and if thinking is a verbal and visual language in our heads, writing is verbal and visual thinking on paper. The act of writing doesn't just convey our thinking but also shapes it. As we write, our brains are busy synthesizing, summarizing, organizing, and determining what is important enough to *think through our fingers*. Frequent short bursts of writing throughout the day give our students more time to think on paper with greater automaticity, fluency, and agency to *discover what they know*.

If you are reading this book, I doubt you need any convincing on the importance of writing as a vehicle for learning. I hope that you find ideas and approaches in this text helpful, not only to increase the volume and stamina of your writers but also to spark their thinking about writing in new ways; and to find their voices as writers and communicate more effectively and confidently. I hope students begin to see how writing can help them tap into their own identity and agency as they explore their thoughts, feelings, and beliefs through writing and responding. It is also my wish that quick writing will encourage our children to be more mindful of the world around them by helping them to tune in and develop a habit of noticing and reflecting.

My Evolution of Quick Writes

I stand on the shoulders of some incredible writing mentors who have shaped *my* thinking about quick writes, though I realize my approach and purpose differ somewhat from theirs. Linda Rief's book *100 Quickwrites: Fast and Effective Freewriting Exercises That Build Students' Confidence, Develop Their Fluency, and Bring Out the Writer in Every Student* (2003) transformed how I thought about writing to discover thinking.

Linda knew many students were often insecure about their writing, so she looked for ways to support them. Quick writes, she noted, "are nonthreatening precisely because they are short and quick, yet focused. . . . When carefully selected so that students can readily relate to them, they give students models to stimulate their thinking about their own topics in concrete and specific ways." The focus of her quick writes were language-rich poems, essays, and vignettes, as well as several thought-provoking drawings. She saw these quick writes as "seeds of ideas, the beginning of a piece to be worked on right away, or at the very least, captured for later use" (Rief 2003, 14).

Other mentors include Donald Graves and Penny Kittle, coauthors of *My Quick Writes: For Inside Writing* (2005). Graves discussed the difference between quick writes and traditional writing prompts: "Quick writes nudge us to discover topics that matter, not to respond to a question that may have nothing to do with our experience. When writing quickly, our own thoughts can surprise us. Quick writes seek diversity, not conformity" (Graves and Kittle 2005, 3).

I wanted to explore how a similar approach to writing could be used in elementary classrooms to help our students write to discover. In addition to using the prose and poetry of others, I wanted to include responding to information and data, sharing opinions and engaging in arguments, analyzing the visual and musical arts, and even reflecting on our sense of self.

The quick writes in this book are intended to increase the volume of writing our students are doing in our classrooms each day and give them practice with narrative, informational, explanatory, opinion, and self-reflective forms of writing. Though we may use the term *quick write* generically, I want to honor and differentiate the purpose and goals of these approaches.

You can simply Google *quick writes* and find ideas for prompts to try out with your students, so why do you need a book? I believe that educators should be purposeful in what we do and understand how our instructional approaches affect student learning. There are many shiny objects vying for our attention on social media and teacher resource sites, all available at the click of a button. We need to be wise consumers of materials, lessons, and approaches that we bring into our classrooms. We need to be the guardians of sound educational practice and protectors of valuable learning time. Random collections of quick writes may invite variety, but

- I want my students to *play with purpose* as they write.

- I want to use the precious time we have wisely.

- I want quick writing to increase the volume and deepen the thinking of my writers.

- I want writing and thinking to become synonymous for my students and help them to build a sense of agency and identity as learners.

How This Book Works

I start each chapter with a quick write that reflects my initial thinking on the chapter. You may notice that the chapters don't always follow these quick writes exactly. That is because writing truly does lead to discovery, and as I explored the approaches and concepts in each chapter and learned from the work of our students, my thinking was frequently stretched and revised.

In the first chapter, I share the rationale for why we use quick writes and how I believe they help the students in our classrooms become not only stronger writers but also more enlightened people. I discuss the concept of fostering intradependent communities to lift the thinking and learning of all within the group, and I share how you can enhance the learning and awareness of your students with a five- to ten-minute investment of daily writing.

In subsequent chapters, I offer a variety of quick write exercises that focus on varied aspects of thinking and writing. You can try them all or focus on areas that would best support your students' needs or your current teaching and curriculum. I offer many examples of quick writes our students have created and take you inside some classrooms of the teachers I work with, who use these daily quick writes in a variety of ways. Though most of the exercises can be adapted and implemented in grades K–6, I also offer a chapter that is designed to meet the unique needs of emergent and primary writers to focus on automaticity and fluency in writing at the letter, word, and sentence levels. I conclude with a chapter of quick writes for teachers to spark our reflective practice and help us to walk the talk of a writer.

I have compiled resources with ideas, templates, and websites and linked to them using QR codes and URLs for quick access throughout the book. These can help get you started until you curate your own collection of sparks that support the specific needs, interests, and goals of your students. A big focus of this book is to help us think purposefully about the work we are asking of our students to maximize our limited time together.

At the end of each chapter, I invite you to quick write a reflection of your thinking or your own ideas for supporting your students or content area. Take what you read and see here and make it your own by tailoring it to the needs of your class. I believe that you and your students could reap great benefits with this small but significant investment of time and energy and possibly find quick writes the most rewarding ten minutes of your day.

Remember, "Life is short. Do stuff that matters."

CHAPTER 1
Why Quick Write?

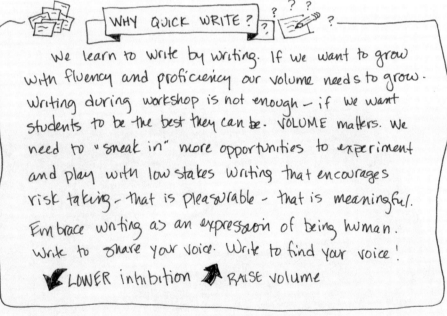

WHY QUICK WRITE? ? ? ?

We learn to write by writing. If we want to grow with fluency and proficiency our volume needs to grow. Writing during workshop is not enough — if we want students to be the best they can be. VOLUME matters. We need to "sneak in" more opportunities to experiment and play with low stakes writing that encourages risk taking — that is pleasurable — that is meaningful. Embrace writing as an expression of being human. Write to share your voice. Write to find your voice!

LOWER inhibition   RAISE volume

Figure 1.1
Quick writes rule!

QUICK GLANCE: Examining our beliefs about writing will guide us in determining how quick writes can help meet student goals and deciding the best selections to address their needs.

Just as some terms in education evolve to take on different meanings from teacher to teacher, my use of the phrase *quick writes* may differ from one that you are familiar with. My working definition for the quick writes in this book is: *Short and frequent bursts of low-stakes writing in response to a stimulus (spark) that do not allow for planning, revising, or overly cautious forethought. They constitute thinking on paper that helps students creatively explore ideas while boosting their volume of writing.* Or, put simply:

Thinking and Inking.

But before we ask "Why quick write?" we should contemplate why we want our students to write at all. I think you would agree that our goal lies far beyond covering standards and curriculum. It isn't to raise scores; it is to raise humans. If our writing instruction doesn't embrace and support this existential goal, I believe we are wasting precious time in our classrooms each day.

Writing to Be Human

Written language seems to be both unique and integral to human nature. It has the power to convey information so that we can learn beyond our personal experiences; to preserve our memories, personally and collectively as a human race; to bring people together and spread awareness of news and events beyond our arbitrary borders. Writing has the power to help us explore, discover, and express our thoughts in a way that is at the heart of being human, and our students need us to teach it in ways that engage and empower them beyond a standardized curriculum.

So, what do many students perceive writing to be? Do they grasp the potential in exploring, recognizing, and tapping into their humanity through writing? Do they contemplate the influence of communicating through written thought? Are they curious to discover where their writing may take them? Or do they see writing as the completion of an assignment, the ticking off of a checklist, and the hope of a good grade? Are they worried more about what *we* as teachers may think, rather than discovering what *they* themselves think? It isn't a binary choice but more likely a continuum of perceptions. At which end of the spectrum do most of your writers fall? Once we have a solid understanding of why we should write, we can begin to focus on the best practices to support that purpose. (See Figures 1.2 and 1.3.)

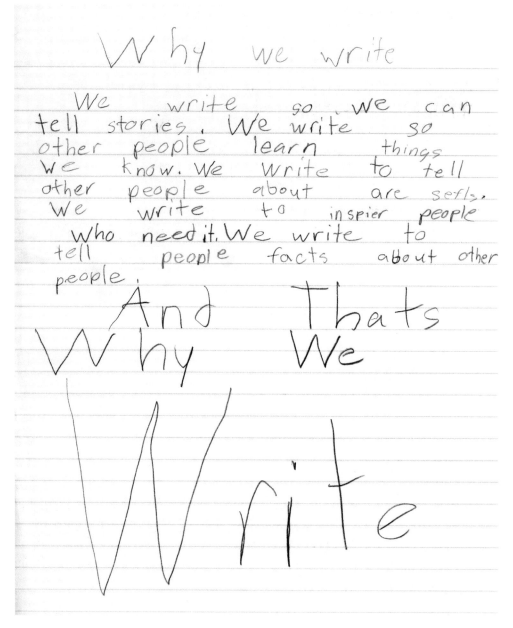

Figure 1.2
Why we write

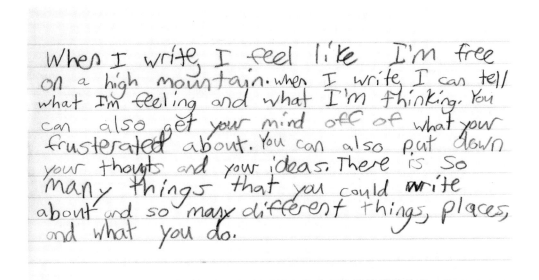

When I write, I feel like I'm free on a high mountain. When I write, I can tell what I'm feeling and what I'm thinking. You can also get your mind off of what your frusterated about. You can also put down your thougts and your ideas. There is so many things that you could write about and so many different things, places, and what you do.

Figure 1.3
When I write . . .

As teachers, we are pummeled by calls to *get back to the basics*—to standardize teaching and quantify learning. However, I believe we are at a critical time in our democracy where teaching plays a crucial role in raising thoughtful, attentive, and curious human beings. A friend reminded me of a quote by George Orwell that best illustrates my sense of urgency: "If you cannot write well, you cannot think well; if you cannot think well, others will do your thinking for you." Students cannot write well without lots of practice. We need to make sure we give them this practice so that others will not do their thinking for them.

Writing for Social-Emotional Learning

The Collaborative for Academic, Social, and Emotional Learning (CASEL) defines social-emotional learning as "the process through which children and adults acquire and effectively apply the knowledge, attitudes, and skills necessary to understand and manage emotions, set and achieve positive goals, feel and show empathy for others, establish and maintain positive relationships, and make responsible decisions." Students need opportunities to build these skills in a safe environment. Classroom discussions and lots of modeling are essential, and I believe quick writes can play a powerful role as well.

Personal challenges such as trauma, poverty, and stress compete with our teaching for students' attention and impact their social-emotional development as well as their academic learning. I have seen firsthand how writing has reframed thinking, offered cathartic release, and challenged perceptions. My relationships with students have been strengthened by getting to know their thoughts, hopes, fears, and experiences from short, unfiltered, and unevaluated bursts of writing.

Creating Lifelong Writers

I have been encouraged by the ongoing movement to create lifelong readers, which I believe has positively influenced our instruction of reading. We want academic reading experiences to more closely mirror real-life reading, so we encourage students to reflect on themselves as readers who choose books, read voraciously, and comprehend more deeply. Similarly, I want to create lifelong writers who write prodigiously and think more keenly.

To achieve these objectives, we need to foster a habit of writing by infusing each day with multiple opportunities to reflect upon, notice, communicate, and respond to ideas. We need to break down the academic wall of writing to bring in a variety of experiences, ideas, purposes, and audiences that stimulates more authentic writing. We need our kids to believe that it is more important what *they* think about their writing than what *we* think if we have any hope of creating lifelong writers. We need them to experience the joy, wonder, and power writing can bring to our lives.

Fostering a Climate of Intradependence

In his book *The 7 Habits of Highly Effective People*, Stephen Covey (2004) talks about the development of personal and interpersonal effectiveness as a maturity continuum. He discusses how we begin life entirely *dependent* on others, but as we grow, we become more inner-directed and self-reliant, or *independent*. Then, as we mature further, we realize that all of nature is *interdependent*, relying on the mutual cooperation of others for the success of a common goal, or even survival. He considers these the paradigms of *YOU*—you take care of me, *I*—I can do it myself, and *WE*—we can do it together, we cooperate.

I believe we can foster another kind of *WE* relationship in our classrooms to inspire our students to become highly effective people. I see *intradependence* as a model that encourages working beside one another in our classrooms as mentors and resources to lift the independent learning goals of all. How does this differ from interdependence? I see it as a subtle but important distinction: The prefix *inter-* means between two or more groups, while *intra-* means within or inside one group. Our goal is to support the learning for all within one group—our classroom.

This aligns with Aristotle's words, "The whole is greater than the sum of its parts." The interaction and connection among individuals produce a combined effect that is greater than the sum of those individuals' contribution. This is known as synergy. An intradependent classroom fosters this synergy. When we share our work, our processes, our approaches with peers, we elevate the thinking of all. We may not be collaborating on the same writing project or for a common outcome or grade, but we can support one another to grow personally, as well as collectively, as writers. When students mentor and teach one another, their confidence increases, as does the confidence of those learning from them. Because quick writes are short and easy to share, their frequency provides ample opportunities to grow and learn from one another.

Aligning Instruction with Our Beliefs

Ultimately, determining if quick writes are valuable to you will require that you reflect on your beliefs about writing and then decide if this approach aligns with them. It is important as educators to develop core principles upon which we base our pedagogy and focus instruction. Ask yourself, "What are my core beliefs? Does my instructional approach support my beliefs? Are there gaps or areas I would like to direct more intention?" Then ask yourself, "What are my students' beliefs about writing? How do my instructional choices influence their beliefs?"

Quick Write Invite

What are *your* core beliefs about writing?

THIS I BELIEVE:
1. Writers get better at writing by *writing*.
2. Writing not only reflects thinking but also shapes thinking.
3. Writing is inextricably tied to emotion, identity, and humanity.
4. Every child needs and deserves an entry point into writing to help them find their voice.
5. We need to expand our definition of writing to realize its full potential.

When I reflect on my beliefs, I am convinced that quick writes are an invaluable part of my daily instruction, not just for writing but for living and learning more generally. I hope you find quick writes within this book that enhance your instruction, align with your core beliefs, and expand your students' beliefs about writing.

The instructional choices we make as teachers and the purposeful use of our time has never been more critical in meeting our students' needs as human beings. I have written this book with both those needs and the constraints of teachers in mind. The goals I propose may sound lofty, but my aim is simple: to provide a purposeful practice in using microbursts of writing each day as a vehicle for thinking and finding our voices.

Benefits of Daily Quick Writes

Many of us teach genre-based units of study that immerse our students in the structure, traits, and skills they need to be successful in a given mode of writing. But however effective a unit of study may be, many teachers tell me they feel this approach can cause their students to miss out on other types of writing. Students can develop tunnel vision about what writing is supposed to be when they are singularly focused on components of a rubric or a learning progression. By developing a habit of daily quick writes, I have observed benefits to students beyond the targeted skills and grades that measure the success of writing instruction.

WHAT SPARKS CAN QUICK WRITING OFFER OUR STUDENTS?
1. Develop valuable "soft skills" beyond literacy
2. Reset students' default approach to writing
3. Strengthen relationships with our students
4. Increase enjoyment of writing

Increasing Low-Stakes Writing

You only get better at something by doing it—a lot! Unfortunately, many of our students don't choose to write independently and are often reluctant to write when it is assigned. Many students report that they don't enjoy writing and that they don't see themselves as good writers. I believe these perceptions often arise when students put a piece of themselves on paper that they know will be graded. For these students the stakes are high, and so are their stress levels. This stress can manifest itself in ways that inhibit expression, thinking, and development of writing skills. Students believe the less writing they do, the less they will be judged.

Grading isn't some evil we are inflicting on our students; it is a simple reality of our accountability system. Schools want to make sure that students are learning and growing, so we need to measure that growth. But not every piece of writing needs to be evaluated or graded. We need to look for a balance between high-stakes and low-stakes writing for our students if we want to increase engagement and volume of writing. (See Figure 1.4 for examples of high- and low-stakes writing.)

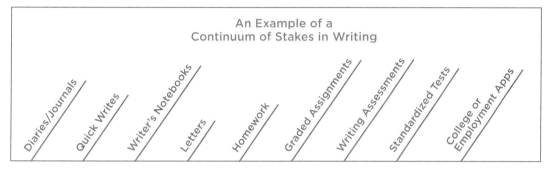

Figure 1.4
Purpose and audience can determine the stakes for writing.

Low-stakes writing is a way for students to practice reflecting, experimenting, and expressing thoughts on paper in a way that is not subject to outside evaluation, criticism, or even suggestions. It is rarely graded because it is not seen as a final product. We can look at it as an opportunity to play with ideas or compose thoughts that no one is going to judge. If we are concerned about someone assessing our work, we may become cautious, careful, and conservative in our attempts. Experimenting can become too risky. Play may not feel safe.

Even though the stakes are low, the benefits can be high. I've had students share poems, comics, and novels they have written just for themselves that were clever, heartbreaking, or bizarre but looked nothing like the work they submitted in class. This was authentic writing that they cared about and went beyond any expectations I had for them as writers.

I recall one student who wrote dark, gothic novellas and poetry outside of class and brought them in to share with me. I sensed she was using this writing to work through fears and experiences in her life. She and I talked a lot about her writing, though she did not want to talk much about herself. The year after she moved to middle school, I received a card from her. I think she wanted me to know her life was changing (see Figure 1.5). Low-stakes writing gave her a voice. (See Figure 1.6 for characteristics of low- and high-stakes writing.)

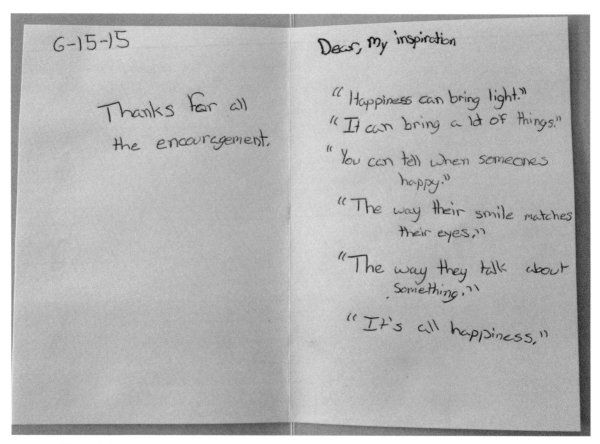

Figure 1.5
Writing empowers students.

Figure 1.6

High- vs. low-stakes writing

HIGH-STAKES WRITING	LOW-STAKES WRITING
Is graded or used as evaluation	Is not graded
Is enhanced through the writing process	Focuses on rehearsal or drafting
Has specific criteria for success	Has no specific criteria for success
Is often in response or related to texts	Is often a personal response or reflection
Is used to demonstrate learning	Often stimulates curiosity and wonder
Focuses on learning to write	Focuses on writing to learn or create
Must adhere to the prompt	May or may not be inspired by a prompt
Is used as a summative assessment	

Developing Important Soft Skills Beyond Literacy

While I believe literacy development is critical, I also believe supporting students' development as human beings is an even higher priority. To address this, I've designed quick writes that encourage students to contemplate big ideas in accessible ways. Whether you call them soft skills or twenty-first-century skills, our students need opportunities to grow as more thoughtful, aware, and responsive citizens in our classrooms and society. Daily quick writes offer a platform for that practice. Let's look at some vital soft skills they support.

CRITICAL THINKING

Critical thinking requires students to be creative, reflective, and flexible. We want them to "think outside the box" and avoid "cookie-cutter thinking" in which there is one right answer, structure, or response (see Figure 1.7). To develop these skills, students need lots of opportunities to grapple with ideas, play around with thoughts, and engage with prompts or problems. Daily quick writes can be the perfect spark for kindling critical-thinking skills. They provide students practice at exploring their own thinking process and, if shared, can allow students to see multiple ways of approaching ideas.

Figure 1.7
Critical-Thinking Skills

CRITICAL-THINKING SKILLS
Logical problem solving
Determining importance and relevance
Making connections between ideas
Thinking flexibly and openly
Evaluating evidence and arguments
Thinking creatively

CREATIVITY

To foster creativity, we have to immerse students in a creative environment. We can hook them with interesting images that stimulate a sense of wonder. We can use prompts that tie in the emotions of the learner. We can spark curiosity by inviting them to wonder and not just answer. We can embrace the *messiness* of writing that isn't revised or edited, simply experienced. We can celebrate the expressive freedom that won't be hindered by evaluation or assessment. We can incorporate art, music, and culture as a vehicle to stimulate thinking. The open-ended nature of a quick write is ideal for encouraging creativity.

COMMUNICATION

The only way to get better at communicating with others, in writing or any other mode of expression, is through purposeful practice. When we help students understand elements of effective communication and give them opportunities to develop their expertise, they can deepen their thinking and convey ideas more efficiently. Quick writes allow them to focus on specific aspects of the content with repeated practice so they can begin to find creative ways to express themselves and engage others.

Part of communicating is also being receptive to others' ideas, to listen with an open mind, and to reflect thoughtfully. In classrooms where students share their quick writes, students have abundant opportunities to practice listening to the ideas of others. They begin to notice what is said—and what is not said. I've designed quick writes for students to respond to music, stories, or one another to encourage more active listening before reacting.

MINDFULNESS

Mindfulness is not some new-age craze; it is merely the ability to focus our awareness on the present moment. Too often our children lack that ability, to the detriment of their well-being. Mindfulness has implications for our social-emotional development as well as our cognitive learning. Our brains are continually being reshaped by experience and thought, and it is our awareness that determines which networks will be strengthened or weakened. Quick writes help students develop purposeful attention to their world and their responses to it, which they can use to make better decisions. Cultivating consciousness with five to ten minutes of purposeful writing is a daily practice in being present, with powerful implications for our students.

COLLABORATION

Collaboration is an essential twenty-first-century skill, both in the classroom and beyond. Some of the quick writes I use are meant to be collaboratively composed, but students can also practice the skill of collaboration as they listen and respond to the writing of others. Each student brings unique perspectives and ideas to the classroom; honoring those differing ideas as valid and valued is a crucial collaboration skill. As previously mentioned, daily quick writes help to foster that intradependent synergy in our classrooms (see Figure 1.8).

Resetting Students' Default Approach to Writing

When we look at student writing, we can often see a pattern of thinking and organization that is routinely expressed. We might notice that students enter a piece of writing in a very predictable way or that their choice of topics or genre structure lacks variety. They may have developed a *default setting*, manifested as an inability to envision any need for revision or to vary the structure and style of their pieces. They can get caught in a rut. Quick writes can help shake things up by offering students new and varied writing interactions.

Do you have students who suffer from writer's block? Quick writes allow writers to initiate a piece of writing each day, sometimes more than once. It's intimidating to stare at a blank page and wonder how to get started, and having daily practice in it helps build student confidence, resetting their default mode of waiting for help or ideas. As Jack London wrote, "You can't wait for inspiration. You have to go after it with a club."

Figure 1.8
Sharing quick writes fosters intradependence.

If writing in our classrooms is limited exclusively to month-long, genre-based, or project-oriented units of study, students get little opportunity to play around with other approaches and reset the default mode; they only have one opportunity to initiate an entry point, consider structure, explore a character or topic, contemplate an ending, and so on. Supplementing our curriculum with quick writes offers our writers dozens of opportunities each month to approach new writing with an open and curious mind.

Quick Writes as Improvisation

Quick writing is not the same as free writing, which allows students to choose their own topics or genres to explore. I wholeheartedly advocate for free writing as well, but the practices differ in that quick writing provides writers with a stimulus or *spark*. It is a form of improvisation that can stretch students' mental writing muscles.

Have you ever listened to improvisational jazz? The musicians create melodies on the spot. They are in a free flow of creativity. Researchers at John Hopkins and Harvard (Lehrer

2009) conducted separate studies to examine the brains of some jazz pianists as they improvised and found that they could suppress the dorsolateral prefrontal cortex of their brains, associated with executive function and self-control, as they played. This allowed them to be less inhibited and more creative. The researchers also found that the musicians were able to activate the medial prefrontal cortex associated with memory, self-expression, and identity, using what they already knew about music to create unique riffs. Many writers try to get into this same zone as they let creative ideas flow onto their papers. As Lehrer (2009) notes, "Scientists argue that expert musicians create new melodies by relying on the same mental muscles used to create a sentence; every note is another word." The same parts of the brain that facilitate jazz improvisations could help us to write more creatively and freely.

If you have ever attended an improv theater, you will see something very similar. Actors are given a basic premise and must work together to spontaneously create scenes with action, reaction, dialogue, and characterizations. Because the cast does not know what audience members may suggest, they cannot plan and organize; they must draw upon what they know and respond. They restrict their analytical thinking and activate their creative thinking. The more varied opportunities for practice they have, the better they get. Similarly, quick writes do not allow for planning, rehearsal, revising, or overly cautious forethought. They stimulate parts of our brains to write in more uninhibited ways using what we already know about writing and the world around us.

As author Donald Murray has said, "Write fast—write badly—so you will write what you don't yet know you knew, and so you will outrun the censor within us all." Our students need playful opportunities to outrun their censors and discover their thinking.

Strengthening Relationships with Students

I have learned so much about my students over the past few years through quick writes. The practice has allowed me to see aspects of their lives, their hopes, their beliefs that I might not have otherwise discovered. Students bring life experiences with them into class that affect their learning, their emotions, and their behavior. We can get valuable insights into who they are as humans, not just as learners, through daily quick writing.

When we share our own quick writes with students, we evolve from a mentor-pupil dynamic to a writer-colleague one. We can build empathy for our writers because we are walking in their shoes. We can appreciate the diversity of ideas from a firsthand perspective.

Figure 1.9
Teachers can quick write along with their students.

Students respect teachers who walk the talk. We increase our credibility and become equal and integral members of our learning communities (see Figure 1.9).

Enjoyment

We can all use more fun in our lives, and we should not turn down opportunities to infuse learning with enjoyment—especially when we are talking about only five to ten minutes a day. Typically, we don't do what we don't enjoy, so we can't expect our students to make writing a habit unless they find joy in it. When it is time for quick writes, students are often eager to pull out their notebooks and share their thinking with classmates (see Figure 1.10).

When we expand our definition of writing to include visuals, word bursts, sketchnotes, or stream of consciousness, we open the door to creative ideas that are enjoyable and accessible to all kids. Students with limited English or emerging writing skills can explore and express their thinking more independently when they are not limited by their literacy proficiency. This independence enhances engagement and enjoyment for writers.

Incorporating visual imagery with verbal information has been found to be beneficial to student learning. Researcher Allan Paivio (2006) hypothesized that verbal and visual information are processed by different parts of the brain. By incorporating words and images, students are stimulating more areas of the brain, which could enhance their learning and increase their chances of recalling information. Anyone who works with primary writers has seen firsthand the power of pictures to help students remember and reread their writing.

Are Quick Writes for You?

If you have students who are reluctant to write, who have difficulty getting started with writing, or who are proficient but stagnant in their growth as writers, quick writes can help. If you would like your students to explore their thinking, reflect on their identity,

Figure 1.10
Enjoyment is a crucial goal for quick writing.

and find their voice, quick writes can help. If you want to get to know your students more intimately, build stronger relationships, and create a supportive writing community, quick writes can help. If you want to cultivate more joy and success in the lives of your writers, quick writes can help. There is so much potential thinking and learning awaiting your students in ten minutes or so a day!

Quick Write Invite

What are you thinking or wondering about quick writes? How could they align with your core beliefs or goals for your students?

CHAPTER 2

How to Use Quick Writes

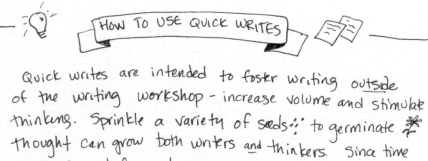

Figure 2.1

My quick write

QUICK GLANCE: Once we determine why we would use quick writes we can select the format or focus that works best for our students.

How Do Quick Writes Differ from Minilessons?

As you go through this book you may notice that many of the *sparks* I use for quick write ideas could be extended into minilessons during writing workshop as well. A more purist interpretation of quick writing may envision stream-of-consciousness thinking on paper in response to some stimulus or prompt, and I certainly offer opportunities for this approach. I have designed the quick writes in this book to inspire thinking from a range of sparks a bit more intentionally. Our elementary writers need lots of writing experience for a variety of purposes, and we *increase* that diversity when we *decrease* the time commitment for each. Short bursts of diverse writing sprinkled through the day can encourage flexibility in thinkers and writers and increase the volume of low-stakes writing our students generate.

By contrast, minilessons provide instruction in a skill or technique that students will then connect to a larger lesson or subsequent piece of writing. Minilessons precede the writing workshop, whereas quick writes stand alone as their own type of writing exercise. There is no expectation that they lead or contribute to a completed piece of writing. They are not tied to a single genre of instruction. They are not evaluated, assessed, or judged by others. Their primary goal may not even be to improve writing skills but to encourage habits of mind, foster awareness and appreciation, or stimulate thinking. They are meant not to replace writing workshop for your students but to supplement the writing you already do with short spurts of thinking on paper.

I've organized the chapters that follow around some focus areas that I think could be enhanced through daily quick writes.

- Chapter 3: Emerging—to develop greater automaticity and fluency at the letter, word, and sentence level for our primary writers

- Chapter 4: Information—to activate prior knowledge, stimulate curiosity, and express opinions from a wide variety of informational sources

- Chapter 5: Appreciation—to expose students to a variety of art in visual, auditory, or verbal formats and invite personal responses as an integral expression of language arts

- Chapter 6: Creativity—to promote more playful practice when composing narrative writing and communication with others

- Chapter 7: Social-Emotional—to nurture mindfulness, encourage metacognitive skills, and foster a mind-set of reflection, motivation, and gratitude

- Chapter 8: Teacher—to inspire and support learning and leadership for all writing teachers through collaboration and reflection

The book wasn't designed to be read cover to cover, so you can dip in and try some quick writes to address specific needs or start with an area that appeals to you. The big idea is that you build a daily habit for writing that increases your students' volume of writing and extends (or moves beyond) your writing curriculum in ways that are engaging and create a broader, more positive perception of writing for students.

Children's book author Sarah Aronson shares some advice she received from her first editor, Deborah Brodie: "Eat dessert first." In other words, write what makes you happy to get started. If you enjoy writing, you will write more. Our students need opportunities to sample writing as a dessert so they can experience how sweet it can be. Quick writes are not the main course of our writing curriculum but samplers that allow for a wide range of experiences and tastes. The wider the variety, the better the chance they will find writing that they enjoy.

Quick Write Schedules

The schedule for incorporating quick writes into your day will depend upon the types and purposes you decide to use. Some teachers start the day with a quick write as an entry task to set an inspirational or collaborative tone for the class—or as exit slips at the end of lessons to use as formative assessments and reflection opportunities. Others find they have short slots in their schedules each day before lunch, recess, or specials that lend themselves to creative microbursts of writing. Still others like to end the day with mindful quick writes that cap off a day of learning and create a positive trajectory for students leaving school.

You may want to consider a predictable schedule to help students anticipate and easily engage in regular quick writes if your students work better with structure. Some teachers vary their daily focus and use quick writes multiple times throughout the day for different purposes. Sometimes these quick writes are spontaneous sparks in response to students, experiences, or events.

WEEKLY FOCUS

Many classrooms I work in choose to select one area of focus per week to give students multiple opportunities to explore their thinking and play with ideas over several days. This can work well when tied to content area material around which students can build schema. A weekly focus can also build confidence in reluctant writers who get several cracks at a quick write. It can also foster intradependence if students have an opportunity to hear from their peers and share ideas that they can then go back and try out for themselves. A weekly focus can support students by creating an anticipatory set to prepare them for writing and perhaps encourage them to take notice of the world outside the classroom in preparation.

A weekly focus may also offer students an opportunity to bring in poems, photos, music, or artifacts during the week that they can use as sparks. This allows our kids to be more invested in the process and helps them to realize that writers get ideas and inspiration from many places in their lives. They don't have to wait for others to prompt or inspire them.

For those teachers who consistently use quick writes as exits slips after lessons, they find it often helps students reflect on their learning and pay closer attention to learning targets or expectations in anticipation of this reflection. This is an effective way in which writing can shape thinking as well as share thinking.

DAILY VARIETY

I work in several classrooms that have a repertoire of daily themes for quick writes. Some are predictably built into the weekly schedule (for example Wondering Wednesdays or Thoughtful Thursdays). You could consider a variety of quick writes during the week based on the areas I've outlined in each chapter to keep things fresh or pique curiosity. Sometimes students love the mystery and ask, "What are we going to quick write about today?" Students could even submit ideas for "Mystery Mondays" or "Wise Words Wednesdays." Let your choices be guided by intention and purpose or a sense of inquisitive experimentation—just write!

Quick Write Tools

The tools we use to compose and collect our ideas influence our composition. Think about your goals for quick writing and seek to intentionally match the tool to the job. You may want to experiment with a variety of formats, utensils, and approaches until you find what best meets your objectives. I'll share some of our most common means for quick writes.

NOTEBOOKS

Quick write notebooks are very popular with teachers and often consist of composition or spiral-bound notebooks housing a vast collection of low-stakes writing that can easily be revisited. The value in keeping these pieces of writing together can be seen when students reread through their notebooks to mine ideas for writing topics or reflection. Because quick writes occur in a such a short window of time, students are often just getting started with an idea when it is time to stop. Their notebooks are great resources for revisiting and expanding on an idea for future writing projects, if *they* choose, or to reflect on a body of thinking on paper.

Quick write notebooks provide students with a visible and chronological history of their thinking and writing over the course of the year that can be encouraging for them as writers. Success begets success, and seeing how much writing they've accomplished can confirm to students that they are indeed writers. An entire notebook of archived writing ideas is perceived as a successful accomplishment (see Figure 2.2).

GOOGLE CLASSROOM

In classrooms with one-to-one computer access, some teachers have set up a Google Classroom for daily quick writes using the assignment feature (see Figure 2.3). This allows us to embed links to music, videos, websites, and other documents that students can use as sparks for their writing. Google Classroom makes it incredibly easy for the teacher to read through each students' responses and allows students to share their work with others in the classroom if they choose. The students can organize files for their quick writes however they want (for example, by trimester, month, topic, and so on).

One caveat is that many elementary students are not yet proficient with keyboarding skills, which can limit the volume of writing they produce on a computer. Some teachers use quick writes as an opportunity for extending students' keyboard practice as well and feel the strategy to be worthwhile. (You may note from some of the students' examples I share in the book that the digital responses are not very lengthy but still insightful and valuable.)

Figure 2.2
Student quick write notebooks

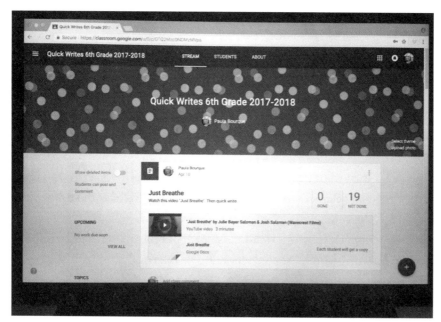

Figure 2.3
Using Google Classroom in our sixth grades for quick writes

Quick Write Collections

Sometimes teachers prefer to curate collections of quick writes by topic or around a prompt so they can celebrate the wide range of responses and ideas. We have created class books (i.e., anthologies) of quick writes that can be shared with others, if the student chooses, as inspiration and celebration. These offer tangible ways to foster intradependence in our classrooms. Remember that the pieces are not revised or edited in preparation for publication; a disclaimer to this effect might precede the work samples if shared with the general public.

WHITEBOARD QUICK WRITES

As varied as quick write purposes and topics are, so too are the tools our students use to compose them. If we want our students to expand their understanding of what writing is, we need to expand our approaches to writing as well. Many envision writing as sitting down with a blank paper in front of them and having to fill it.

Several teachers I work with use their whiteboards as canvases for quick writing (see Figure 2.4). Each morning, they post a prompt on the whiteboard and invite students to write a response as an entry task for the day. Some of these quick writes are quite short, perhaps a few words long, while others could be several sentences long. The idea is for students to share their thinking or opinions in writing as a community. Whiteboard quick writes allow teachers and students to reflect on individual responses as well as contemplate collective classroom thinking. This way of sharing can build an intradependent environment by respectfully honoring the responses of those who may have differing opinions and ideas. They are ephemeral, however (unless we snap some photos!), marking our thinking for this moment, and then they are gone. You can find dozens of ideas by Googling "whiteboard prompts," and I encourage you to consider the purpose when choosing from the abundant online options.

Quick Write Formats

I will share some snippets from classrooms to help you visualize the context and possible approaches to quick writing. When we first introduce a new quick write spark or prompt, we should do so as briefly as possible so that students can use the bulk of time to write and share. Introductions should convey the purpose with our students. Why do we want them to reflect on their mind-set? How will writing about music benefit them? What

Figure 2.4

Starting the day with a positive quick write

can they learn from responding to poetry? We want students to explicitly understand the connection between their quick writing and their learning, understanding, or identity.

The basic format of a quick write is as follows:

- About a minute to introduce the spark

- Up to five minutes of writing

- Up to five minutes of sharing (as appropriate)

Quick Write Directions

There are no standardized directions for teaching or assigning quick writes, but I usually start by telling students: "Quick writes are thinking on paper. The idea is to try to start right away and write the whole time. Let the ideas flow from your brain, down your arm, through the pencil (or keyboard), and onto the paper. If you don't know what to write, you could jot down—'I'm not sure what I think about . . .' or 'I'm having a hard time deciding what I want to say first about . . .' Often the ideas will come to you as you write those words. If not, you are still practicing putting what is in your head on paper."

I talk to students about writing as an act of discovery—how a fairly simple idea can often lead to new ideas. I have shared the idiom of "priming the pump" to illustrate this concept. I tell them older mechanical pumps used to require a small amount of water to get them started properly. A small amount of writing might help get students primed for more in-depth thinking or extensive pieces of writing in the same way. I also share the following quotes to make my point: "I write because I don't know what I think until I read what I say" (Flannery O'Connor), "How do I know what I think until I see what I say?" (E. M. Forster).

I talk to students about building up stamina for writing, explaining that the act of keeping their pencils moving helps with that goal. I tell them it's okay to stop in the middle of a sentence or even a word when the time is up, and that there are many authors who intentionally do this so that they have a starting point the next time they write.

Quick Write Sharing

Katie Wood Ray is one of my heroes in writing instruction. I love this quote of hers: "With a room full of authors to help us, teaching doesn't have to be so lonely" (2002). Though she was referencing mentor texts by published authors, I think she would agree that students and their writing can be mentors for one another as well. If we embrace this stance, we open up a world of possibilities for learning from one another; this is the essence an intradependent classroom. We need to make time each day for students to share their work with one another. This is doable because quick writes are short and the sharing will not take long.

Most kids love to share, especially younger students. Being able to share our own writing is only part of the purpose of sharing; it is equally important to listen and notice. Intradependence, in which the thinking of one stimulates the thinking of all, calls for give *and* take. This may require some practice and explicit teaching. We can mix things up, sharing with a partner, in a small group, or as a whole group depending on what's most appropriate.

To promote active listening and analysis of shared work, we can scaffold our students to critically connect their writing to that of their peers with conversation stems, which encourage students to compare or contrast their thinking with others. Researchers have found strategies that engage students in comparative thinking had the greatest effect on student achievement (Marzano, et al. 2001). You could encourage students to use some of the following stems as they take turns sharing:

- My thinking/writing is similar to _____'s because . . .

- My thinking/writing is different from _____'s because . . .

- I agree with _____'s thinking because . . .

- I respectfully disagree with _____'s thinking because . . .

These kinds of stems also foster a collaborative climate that is a big part of our social-emotional learning goals. We occasionally use American Sign Language during shares to increase engagement and connection: We use the sign for *same* if someone shared a similar thought to our own and *idea* to signal that someone had a good idea that differed from our own (see Figure 2.5).

Teacher responses are as important as students' for fostering intradependence and maintaining the low-stakes focus of quick writes. We want to avoid evaluative language, and that's not easy. Comments such as "I like that" or "Nice one" may seem supportive, but they raise the stakes in ways we may not intend. The goal isn't for students to please others but for them to freely respond and see where their thoughts may take them. We don't want students to wonder, "Will they like this? Is mine good?" There is no *right* response to quick writes, and our feedback needs to convey that. Here are some nonevaluative responses we have tried:

- "Thank you." (or "We appreciate you sharing your thinking with us.")

- Moment of silence (close your eyes, let it sink in, give the student a nod)

- Notice and name ("You chose to write about _____." "You used sensory language.")

- Question ("What made you choose that?" "Did anyone else have similar thinking?")

- Nonverbal (using finger snaps for poetry, sign language to signal same/different thinking)

Figure 2.5
Sharing our quick writes stimulates more thinking.

It is important to realize that sharing isn't always appropriate. Sometimes students are reflecting on very personal ideas, experiences, or even their own identities. We need to be protective of their privacy and realize the best audience for some quick writes may be the students themselves.

Get Started!

At this point, don't overthink it and allow perfect to be the enemy of good. Find ten minutes in your day and try it for a month. What do you notice about the writing? About your students?

Quick Write Invite

Where could you fit more writing into your day?

What tools and formats would work best for your students?

CHAPTER 3
Emerging Quick Writes: Automaticity for Primary Writers

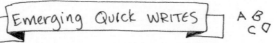

Emerging Quick WRITES   A B C D

Much of our youngest writers' working memory is tied up with the complex task of encoding. Focused attention is directed at the letter and word level. We can design quick writes that meet them where they are to develop automaticity that could then free up some 'bandwidth'—that would allow them to compose more fluently. Keep the focus on process not product. Practice and play with lots of low stakes writing. Take time to learn from one another as a community of writers.

Figure 3.1
My quick write

QUICK GLANCE: Though primary writers can respond to most quick writes in this book, offering options that meet them at their developmental level can spark automaticity and increase volume.

When our youngest students write, their working memory may be so overloaded with phonological processing, spatial planning, letter formation, print concepts, and use of conventions that it can be hard for them to hold on to and retrieve their composed ideas. Early on, nothing is fluent. Everything requires conscious attention, and our brains don't multitask very well. We can free up a bit of that working memory with some quick writes designed to build fluency by focusing on automaticity at the letter or word level before expecting stamina at a more complex sentence or story level.

These quick writes are designed to meet our students where they are in their writing development. I am proposing not a linear progression from letters to words to sentences but rather some playfully purposeful writing time in which students can focus on smaller units of writing to develop proficiency. I place a greater emphasis on the process of thinking on paper with ease and confidence than I do on the final product created. These short pieces won't be evaluated, edited, or revised; they stand as the evidence of thinking and development for each learner. They are more about conveying ideas and process than stories and experiences.

We increase their volume of writing practice by sprinkling multiple opportunities for it throughout each day. We cultivate an understanding that writing time is *any* time we want to think on paper, whether we are thinking about letters, words, or more complex ideas. Quick writes are not intended to replace the writing workshop. They are a way to boost volume and practice with fun and focus.

I do not want to conflate automaticity with speed. A quick write is not a race; it's a space for students to think on paper freely. We want students to get *in the zone* and undergo a state of flow for a few moments. We want them to experience a sense of satisfaction that comes from noticing their process and being a writer. We want to encourage a foundation for mindfulness as writers.

BUILDING A SOLID FOUNDATION

Just like any new skill, the more practice we get using language to share and reflect on our thinking the more proficient we become. However, before our younger students can become competent thinkers on paper, they need to become more proficient thinkers in general. I am inspired by educator James Britton, who contends that writing "floats on a sea of talk." Before expecting students to build writing fluency with quick writes, we must give them opportunities to build thinking fluency with short and frequent bursts of conversation.

Many teachers already use turn-and-talk and class discussions throughout the day. We can make such thinking visible as we model the link between thinking and writing on paper, showing students how to record their thoughts and demonstrating how writing influences thinking. As Tom Newkirk (2018) has tweeted, "Fluency in writing comes from self-prompting. We write a sentence and it prompts another—and another. Soon we have a perpetual motion machine." We can build this fluency with our emergent writers when we model and practice how one word or idea can prompt another—and another. Quick writes can be a useful tool for this task.

We want our youngest writers to approach their writing with courage and curiosity. If we can lay a foundation for "thinking and inking" before they become too intimidated to write, perhaps we'll have fewer students who struggle to get started. If we infuse more variety of purposes or audiences into students' writing, we present students with a broader repertoire for composing more flexibly.

Low-stakes writing can prevent anxiety in younger writers and lower it in older ones. Students need frequent opportunities to write without any expectation of fixing or changing anything if they are to build strong identities as writers. Authentic writing is legitimate *as it is*. We aren't neglecting writing instruction; we are carving out time for exploration and play.

Think about the moves students make playing basketball at recess versus at officiated games. They travel, double-dribble, or foul, but they may astonish us with their athleticism. They have no anxiety about breaking the rules. They are building identity and skill with unfettered practice. We must trust that our writers can do that, too.

Fostering Intradependence

One of the key aspects of quick writes is brevity. Keeping the writing short allows more time for sharing. It is through sharing that possibilities become visible to our writers. As I've said, the power of intradependence is rooted in a simple maxim: "stronger together." We can grow better individually when we are part of a collaborative community. We need to remind students that we don't share to simply showcase our own ideas but to build on the ideas of others. We want to see sharing not as a writing contest but rather as a writing fest where we celebrate and learn from all writers.

To help students contemplate similarities and differences with ideas or structures, we might ask the following questions:

- Who learned something new today?

- Who heard or saw something that they want to try some time?

- Who heard or saw something that was similar to their thinking?

Using stems that promote noticing can help students reflect as well as develop a growth mind-set. We set an expectation that we are receptive to new ways of thinking and expression and that our classroom community can help us explore them.

Emergent Quick Writes

Quick writing at the emergent level encourages students to share their thinking in the manner that works best for them. We honor their responses and encourage the process as much as the product.

LEVELS OF PROCESSING

It was through my Reading Recovery training that I realized just how many levels of processing our students must engage in as they read and write. Both reading for comprehension and writing for meaning are particularly difficult if students are stuck trying to answer questions like "What sound do I hear?" "What letter makes that sound?" "How do I make that letter?" "What's the next sound?" "What word was I writing?" and "What did I say?"

LETTER AND WORD LEVELS

These quick writes invite students to respond at a letter or word level while also allowing for differentiation with students who can do more. As primary teachers, we have expanded our definition of writing to include pictures, scribbles, or letter-like marks as legitimate forms of written expression for emergent writers. Most writers don't stay at the letter level for long because they are naturally eager to expand their knowledge of how words work. Once they achieve some automaticity with letter-sound relationships, they progress quite quickly.

Mystery Letter

We use the Mystery Letter strategy orally first, then turn it into a quick write spark. We reveal a "mystery letter" and ask students to think about the sound the letter makes. Then we ask students to let their brains think of as many words as they can that start with that letter sound. When we do this activity orally, students turn and talk to partners, taking turns for two to three minutes. When we do it as a quick write, students write the mystery letter in the center of their paper and then quickly draw or doodle things that start with that sound, for about five minutes. We then ask them to label their picture, if they can, with at least the beginning sound (which just so happens to always be the mystery letter). You'd be surprised how many times we have heard students exclaim, "Hey, they all start with T!" (See Figures 3.2a and 3.2b for examples.)

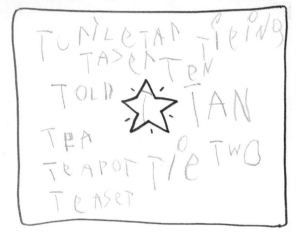

Figure 3.2a and 3.2b
Mystery Letter quick writes allow for differentiation of writing skills.

Some students choose to skip the drawing and focus on brainstorming words that begin with the mystery letter, the foundation for alliteration. It is fascinating to try to discern trains of thought that steer writers from one word to another and to watch kids' faces as they make those discoveries. I see this as the perpetual motion machine Newkirk speaks of. (Figure 3.3 shows more examples of quick writes at the word level.)

Mystery Letter Quick Write To help strengthen letter-sound knowledge and to give students practice at brainstorming what they know, present them with a "Mystery Letter of the Day" and invite them to write that letter in the center and then quick write as many words as they know that begin with that letter (or sound). Younger students may draw images and/or label (at least with the beginning letter)

Figure 3.3

These quick writes spark a variety of strategies for brainstorming and writing at a word level.

Label Maker

As with the Mystery Letter activity, this quick write asks students to make a quick drawing (from a variety of ideas) and then label what they can in their picture quickly and confidently. These are not detailed drawings, though students may later revisit and revise them. We then tell students, "Now we want you to label as many things in your picture as you can for the next five minutes. Don't worry about book spelling; just think about what letters and words you would use to label those parts of your picture." (See Figure 3.4.)

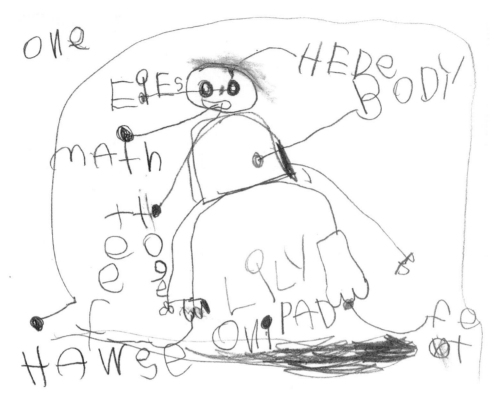

Figure 3.4
Labeling as quick writes for emergent writers

To save time with the drawing, or to increase the available images that could be labeled, we can share our own pictures, photos, or images so students can focus on building letter-sound automaticity and vocabulary. Keep in mind that supplying pictures doesn't provide insight into the students' schema around a topic the way brainstormed drawings may, though it can still provide opportunities to expand vocabulary, invite curiosity, and stimulate thinking while practicing encoding.

Recently I took a photo of Brandi Grady's kindergarten classroom and ran it through a filter that created a line drawing of the image. I shared it with the students and challenged them to label objects in the picture. Brandi and I reminded the students to be brave writers, unafraid to spell words on their own. For ten minutes, students were mesmerized by locating, naming, and labeling items with their best "brave" spellings. When they were done, all were eager to share their labels with one another (see Figure 3.5).

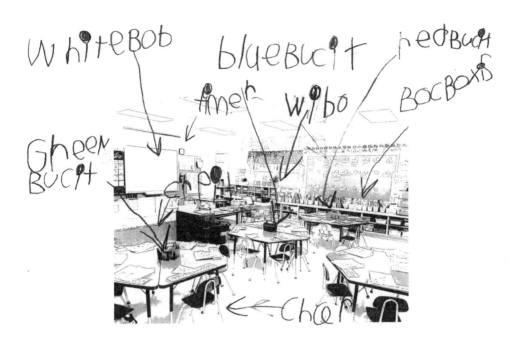

Figure 3.5
Kindergarteners label their classroom.

Word Bursts

As students begin building their personal word banks in writing, we use quick writes to spark practice in recalling and writing these "knowns" and "almost knowns." The key to keeping this activity low-stakes and enjoyable is in how we approach it: "You all have been learning to write so many words lately. We are going to do a Word Burst where you'll write down as many words as you can for just three minutes. Let your brain think about all the words you usually write and jot them down." Then we stand back, observe, and let the students write. Who seemed to work independently and confidently? Who was reluctant or felt the need to copy? I've noticed that some teachers use lined paper and others do not; consider how the format of the paper may influence how and what students write.

When and if students share, it is essential to keep the focus on the process and not the product. We don't want this to become a competition to see who writes the most. We want students to contemplate *their* process—how they chose the words they did and what strategies they thought about. We help them reflect on their process by asking the following questions:

- How did you choose the words you wrote?

- Did any words make you think of new words?

- Did somebody have a different way of choosing words?

- Who was able to write the whole time?

- What were you thinking about while you wrote?

Some students' processes will be meticulous and careful, whereas other students will write with reckless abandon. Some will choose high-frequency words or names, others will explore how words work to generate more ideas, and still others will work on letter-sound connections or letter strings. Looking at these students' Word Bursts, what do you notice about their process (see Figures 3.6a–3.6c)? Over time, students begin building up a significant repertoire for generating words and taking risks when we celebrate their attempts rather than their accuracy or volume.

Figures 3.6a, 3.6b, and 3.6c
First graders' three-minute Word Bursts

Sentence Level

Once students have acquired some fluency at the word level, they have greater working memory to focus on syntax and create sentences that convey their thoughts and ideas more efficiently. Students need the ability to carry a sentence in their mind while they dip down to the letter or word level before they can keep ideas together to create sentences that build and explore concepts.

PIGGYBACK SENTENCES

Here's how we introduce this quick write to students: "When you give a piggyback ride, you pick someone up and bring them along with you. You go together. Sometimes we might write sentences with ideas that don't go together. Today we are going to see if you can write a sentence or two that can piggyback on the one we give you. The sentences need to go together." We then provide students with a starter sentence, or they choose one from their own writers' notebooks. We encourage writers to use the following prompts:

- What happens next?

- What am I thinking?

- How can I describe that?

- What do I see, hear, smell, feel, and so on?

Remember Newkirk: "Fluency in writing comes from self-prompting. We write a sentence, and it prompts another." Playing with this quick write sparks self-prompting thinking and behaviors that support writing fluency. When we share our piggyback sentences with one another, students can begin to internalize the concept of revision as they see and hear so many options and ideas. (See Figure 3.7.)

Quick Writes for Any Age or Stage

Once our primary students have some confidence and fluency as writers, we begin to incorporate many of the quick writes I share in subsequent chapters into our primary classrooms. These can align with content area learning, appreciation of the arts, social-emotional development, and narrative writing the way quick writes for older writers do.

Figure 3.7

Piggyback quick writes encourage writers to "tell us more."

Informational Quick Writes

We use informational quick writes with our primary students to activate prior knowledge, build schema, and gain insights into their understandings and/or misconceptions.

KINDERGARTEN: PRIOR KNOWLEDGE

Meagan Mattice's kindergarten students are about to begin a study of frogs in the spring. Meagan wants to build some excitement about the unit and see what her students know about frogs. She invites them to quick write by saying, "Just take ten minutes and write down what you know about frogs. We all know different things, and we all write in different ways. You don't have to tell us everything—just write what you can in the next ten minutes." (See Figures 3.8a and 3.8b.)

Jenna Sementelli's kindergarteners are embarking on a study of butterflies. During a discussion, students eagerly share their personal experiences. Jenna taps into their engagement. "Sounds like you guys know quite a bit about butterflies. I'm going to give you a piece

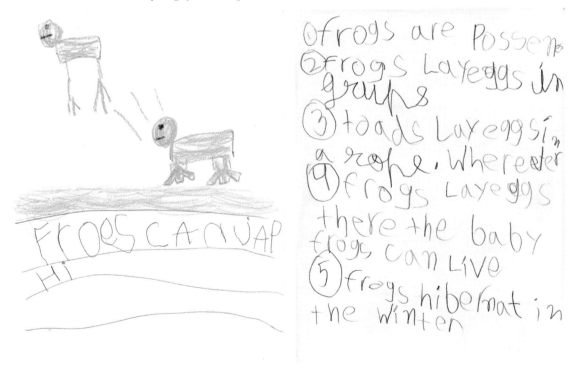

Figures 3.8a and 3.8b
Range of kindergarten quick write responses and organization of frog facts

of paper, and I want you to draw and label what you know about where butterflies live. Picture where you've seen butterflies, and think about what is there. That is a butterfly's habitat, or home. What do you know about a butterfly's habitat?" (See Figures 3.9a and 3.9b.) Students' responses vary in terms of detail and prior knowledge, giving Jenna an idea about their collective schema and writing skills upon which to build her lessons.

As students in both Meagan and Jenna's classes share their work, we hear comments bubbling up in the classroom: "Oooh, I knew that!" "They do?" "What does that mean?" Many are eager to go back and add more details to their writing. They are building schema and excitement around their science units through simple quick writes that allow them to think and ink in small bites.

These teachers don't just use quick writes before introducing units of study. They regularly schedule Write About It Wednesdays or Focus Fridays in which they give students a topic, a picture, or even a word and ask them to share what they know about it. Sometimes they'll invite students to write about something they could teach to others, setting students up as experts in the classroom. Informational quick writes help students to both value what they know and build expertise. They are an excellent springboard for discussion and inquiry, and they provide frequent opportunities to transfer learning of concepts to other topics. Note, for example, how the "expert" in Figure 3.10 transfers his knowledge about habitats to turtles and how the one in Figure 3.11 seeks to clarify that there are "certain kinds of sharks in the ocean."

Figures 3.9a and 3.9b
Kindergarteners quick write by drawing and labeling butterfly habitats.

Figure 3.10
Quick write labeling turtle habitats

Figure 3.11
Kindergarteners quick write to activate prior knowledge and build schema about the ocean.

FIRST GRADE: COMPARE AND CONTRAST

We can use quick writes to encourage and support comprehension strategies as students engage with informational texts or explore content area concepts.

Meg Dyer's first graders are about to begin a social studies unit on the economic idea of wants and needs. Students discuss those terms in a whole group. Meg wants to see what her students think, so she gives them a quick write task to list or draw and label their "wants" on one side and "needs" on the other. Some students seem to have a solid grasp of the abstract concept (see Figure 3.12a) while others still need some clarification (see Figure 3.12b). This quick write helps Meg assess which students need more support and which could offer peer help.

Figures 3.12a and 3.12b
Quick writes let us see how well students grasp concepts.

FIRST GRADE: BRAINSTORMING

As Meg's first graders work on researching topics of interest for an informational unit, she invites them to quick write what they already know about their chosen topics. She can see that her students have varying levels of knowledge and different formats for brainstorming their information (see Figures 3.13a–3.13c). Meg gains valuable insight into how her students recall and organize information from this short burst of writing.

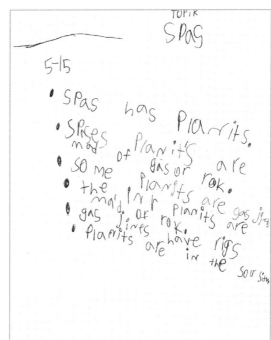

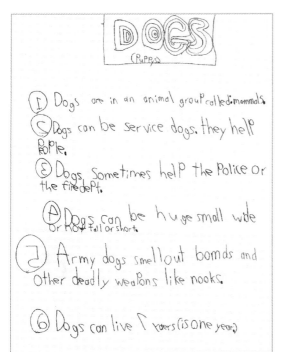

Figures 3.13a, 3.13b, and 3.13c
Quick writes let us see how students organize their thinking.

FIRST GRADE: QUESTIONING

To encourage a sense of curiosity with her first graders, Meg invites them to think about questions they would ask a Pilgrim if they could go back in time. Meg was able to quickly see some misconceptions students had, as well as what they considered valuable information to discover. Even distinguishing the difference between questions and comments is a skill that quick writing can help to reinforce. (See Figures 3.14a and 3.14b.)

Figures 3.14a and 3.14b
First graders quick write questions for Pilgrims in a variety of ways.

Reading Response Quick Writes

Quick writes in response to poetry or stories can be as prevalent in primary grades as they often are in the middle grades. I'll emphasize again that students need lots of opportunities to respond orally before we can expect them to respond fluently in writing. Quick writing doesn't replace turn-and-talk or class discussions; it supplements those conversations by having students think on paper instead of aloud.

POETRY

We read a lot of nursery rhymes and short poems to our kindergarten and first-grade classrooms. Do you ever wonder what students are thinking about as we read? We are so familiar with some of the texts that we might assume students share our interpretations or visualizations. After offering a poem, we can ask our students to quick write about what they were thinking or wondering. Sometimes they make connections and ask questions. Sometimes they surprise you (see Figure 3.15).

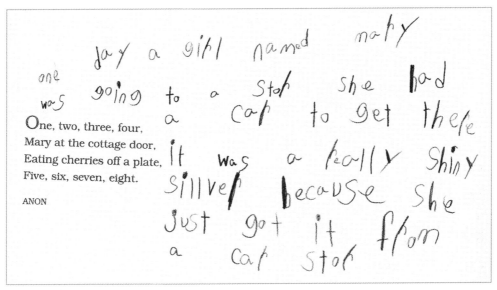

One, two, three, four,
Mary at the cottage door,
Eating cherries off a plate,
Five, six, seven, eight.

ANON

Figure 3.15
There are no "right" responses with quick writes.

LITERATURE

Our primary classrooms are awash with stories. The number of responses we can invite our students to quick write is almost limitless, but remember that a little goes a long way. Writing can be laborious for some of our young writers, so we want to be judicious with our invitations for them to respond in writing. Sometimes we want students to just enjoy a story and maybe talk about it with a friend or draw a picture of what they visualize. The more open-ended our invitations, the more we may learn about our kiddos. Some of the best responses spring from the following questions:

- What are you thinking?

- What are you wondering?

- What are you feeling?

Students can keep their own reader's response notebooks to quick write in private, or teachers could ask if they'd like to share their writings in collections or displays that celebrate a featured book (see Figure 3.16). Just remember that this is low-stakes writing that we don't want students to edit and revise and that their responses are authentic and valid as is.

Quick Wrap

Writing for emergent and primary writers uses up a lot of cognitive bandwidth. Our older writers function on autopilot for many of the writing tasks that our younger writers need to consciously attend to. The metacognitive process of primary writers includes internal

Figure 3.16

A first grader responds to the book *Love* by Matt de la Peña.

conversations such as "What letter makes that sound?" "How do I make that letter?" "Where do I put that letter?" "What's the next letter?" "Hmm, what word am I writing?" and "Oh wait, what was I trying to say?" They need lots of opportunities to write so they can develop automaticity and fluency. Volume matters, yet our young students often don't have the necessary physical or mental stamina to write for long periods of time. We can provide practice with shorter bursts of writing that meet them where they are in their development and give them time to play with ideas without the worry of "doing it right."

Quick Write Invite

What are the most significant needs of your emergent writers?

How could quick writing support those needs? Those writers?

CHAPTER 4

Informational Quick Writes: Knowledge, Wonder, and Opinion

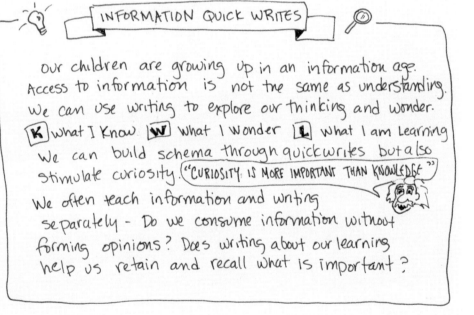

INFORMATION QUICK WRITES

Our children are growing up in an information age.
Access to information is not the same as understanding.
We can use writing to explore our thinking and wonder.
[K] what I Know [W] What I Wonder [L] what I am Learning
We can build schema through quickwrites but also
stimulate curiosity. "CURIOSITY IS MORE IMPORTANT THAN KNOWLEDGE"
We often teach information and writing
separately - Do we consume information without
forming opinions? Does writing about our learning
help us retain and recall what is important?

Figure 4.1

My quick write

QUICK GLANCE: Informational quick writes help students process information to construct personal meaning, spark curiosity, and form opinions.

Information Avalanche

If we want to infuse a greater volume of writing into our students' lives, we need to think beyond our literacy block and contemplate opportunities to incorporate writing into other areas of instruction every single day. Quick writing across content areas can increase the volume of writing while deepening student thinking. Frequent quick writes in response to informational sources can help our students tune in more keenly and create personal meaning from a vast world of factual material. We shouldn't limit students' experience with informational writing to genre studies; instead, we can integrate it throughout the day as a tool to spark their curiosity and help their learning stick.

Buckminster Fuller, an American visionary inventor, developed the concept of Knowledge Doubling Curve. He observed that up until 1900 human knowledge doubled approximately every 100 years, but by 1950 had begun to double every twenty-five years. Fuller referred to this tendency as the "Knowledge Doubling Curve." Some estimate that human knowledge is currently doubling about every thirteen months and is on track to double every twelve *hours* (Schilling 2013). How precise these estimates are is uncertain, but we cannot dismiss the impact of an information avalanche on our society.

Access to information is not the same as understanding. It is imperative that students leave our schools with the capacity to evaluate, synthesize, and apply the information they encounter to lead better lives. We want them to comprehend the information (the *what*) while also appreciating its relevance (the *so what*). Our focus cannot be on recall alone; we must also emphasize relevance and application. We can start by building in a consistent daily practice of reading, viewing, and writing to information among students.

We cannot be satisfied that one or two units of study on informational or opinion writing during the school year will meet our students' needs. Often these units are taught as separate modes of writing although we rarely read informational writing without forming some opinions. Reading and writing are all about making meaning, and this will always be somewhat subjective. Quick writes allow us to experiment with different sources of information and ways of responding to it because we do not need to invest a lot of time teaching or grading it. We can devote our time to exploration and expression; a lower-stakes approach that may encourage riskier, flexible, or more outside-the-box thinking.

Quick Writes as K-W-L

K-W-L (Ogle 1986) was designed as a reading strategy to help students comprehend informational texts. The teacher creates a three-columned chart with the headings *K* (what I *k*now), *W* (what I *w*ant to know), and *L* (what I *l*earned) for students to fill in (see Figure 4.2). The *K* and *W* were intended as prereading strategies to activate schema and stimulate engagement; the *L* was used to track new learning during or after reading. This is a tried and true strategy based on constructivist theory: By linking new information to prior knowledge, our comprehension becomes subjective and personal. What we already know about something influences how we perceive and synthesize incoming information. To create lasting understanding, new knowledge needs something to *stick to*—our schema.

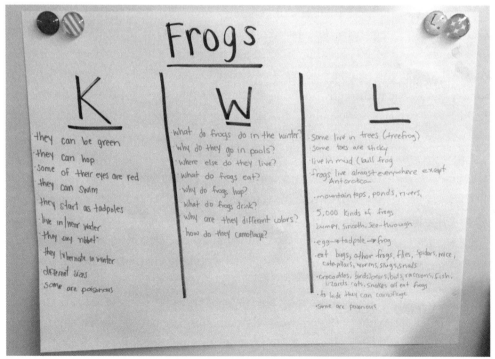

Figure 4.2

We can use the K-W-L framework to craft quick write opportunities.

The K-W-L format is a temporary scaffold for framing and organizing information, and we can use the same structure for informational quick writes. You won't find discrete K-W-L focuses for many of these quick writes, which sometimes combine the three components (discussed further in the following sections). Fundamentally, we want our students to become more aware of what they know, what they wonder, and what they are learning. We want our students to understand that while learning often results from a concentrated unit of study, it also happens daily while reading, listening, observing, and experiencing events mindfully.

WHAT I KNOW

Many teachers use quick writes before embarking on content area topics to increase awareness for both students and themselves. These activities activate students' prior knowledge about the subject to help build a foundation for new learning and provide teachers with insights into students' schema and any misconceptions they may have to guide instruction.

Because students have a short amount of time—usually about five minutes—to brainstorm what they know, quick writes provide critical insights into what was easily retrievable and memorable to them. These accessible "knowns" create a more solid and meaningful foundation upon which to construct new learning. When given the opportunity to share with classmates, many students have aha moments of remembrance or insight that become anchors for learning. These shares highlight the value of fostering a culture of intradependence based on collective knowledge.

WHAT I ~~WANT TO KNOW~~ WONDER

I would prefer to associate the *W* in K-W-L with the word *wonder* because it reflects more of a natural curiosity in the learner than a course of action for learning. This may seem like a subtle distinction, but I have observed a difference in responses when I ask students "What do you want to know?" versus "What do you wonder?" Perhaps the first question makes them feel like they are committing to uncovering answers or conducting research, while the second is an invitation to be curious. Regardless of how you phrase it, quick writing can be an excellent method for encouraging and celebrating our students' sense of wonder.

We don't want to limit our wondering to *before* we learn about something but to foster a stance of inquiry *as* we learn and even *after* our school-based learning is completed. We can stimulate a thirst for knowledge each time we ask students, "What are you wondering now?" Reminding students that there is always more you can learn, that we are never done learning, is critical to developing a growth mind-set.

WHAT I AM LEARNING (FORMATIVE ASSESSMENTS)

Quick writes are a great tool for formative assessments. Often the term *assessment* gets a bad rap because it seems divorced from instruction, but formative assessments *drive* instruction. They allow students to demonstrate their knowledge and skills before, during, or after a lesson. We use them to modify teaching to improve learning.

Quick writes work well as formative assessments because they are short activities embedded in the learning process. Teachers use them to contemplate who may need more support, what misconceptions need addressing, or how deep students' knowledge bases are. They are also powerful markers in a student's learning history that support the development of a growth mind-set—if we give students an opportunity to revisit and reflect.

Teachers who use quick writes as exit slips or reflections have a gold mine of information they can use to determine how well their teaching resulted in learning. Students who quick write about what they have learned have an opportunity to process that information again using multiple parts of their brain. As neurologist Judy Willis notes, "When writing is incorporated in learning and assessment, there is increased opportunity to produce the ideal situation for active, attentive learning because students value creative problem solving or creative production" (Willis 2011). Shorter, more frequent opportunities for informational writing can help make learning stick.

Content Area Learning

Reflecting on our thinking and learning, either orally—such as a turn-and-talk—or with quick writes, can help us better grasp and integrate ideas. Quick writes leave a residue of learning that can be revisited for further reflection in a way that discussions do not. They document our thinking while also shaping it. Deciding what to jot down requires the learner to synthesize and summarize quickly. Regular quick writes can spark the expectation within students that they're supposed to take something from what they write. This anticipation can help increase active engagement and participation in a more self-directed manner.

Jess Walling's fourth graders are learning about the three branches of government. She does an introductory lesson that provides an overview. The next day she asks them to quick write what they know about the three branches, finding that most students have a basic understanding (see Figure 4.3). For the next few weeks, they continue a more in-depth study. As Jess concludes the unit, she again asks the students to quick write for ten minutes what they know about the three branches of government (see Figure 4.4). She wants her students to have a visible learning history as they compare their quick writes. All students were able to observe growth in their knowledge of the topic and feel successful. They didn't compare themselves to others or to a standard for this task to measure their progress, only to their own prior understanding.

THE 3 BRANCHES OF GOVERNMENT

The 3 branches of governmen is 1,Legislative 2,Executive 3, Judicial. The Judicial is the Supreme Cort, and justices. They decides is laws are fair. Legislative, has Congress, Senators and Representatives. Executive is The President, Vice President, and the cabinet members. Executive makes surh that laws are caried for. Also Legislative makes the laws

Figure 4.3

Quick write at the beginning of a unit on the branches of government

Branches of Government!

There are three branches of Government. the Executive, Judichal, and Legislative branches. The Executive branch is the President, Vice President, and Cabnet members. The Executive branch is aloud to vito bills and can direct the militaty. The Executive branch can also carry the laws. The next branch is Legislative branch. The Legislative branch is dived into two groups the house of Repusentatives and the Senet. They are aloud to impeach the president, and they can make the laws. The Leglislative branch is also abud to declare war. The last branch is Judishuil. They are the supreme cort and other small corts. They make shur that laws are fair. There are also nine justices in the supreme cort. And no branch is more powerful then any other.

Figure 4.4

Quick write after completing a unit on the branches of government

Erin Whitish's fifth graders are learning about the water cycle as part of a science unit. There is a test coming up at the end of the week, and she is concerned that some students aren't prepared. We give her students an opportunity to reflect and become more aware of their current understanding with a ten-minute quick write to explain the steps of the water cycle. Some students know the concepts but not the vocabulary, some tell it as a sequence of events, and others use a mixture of text and visuals to explain the process (see Figure 4.5).

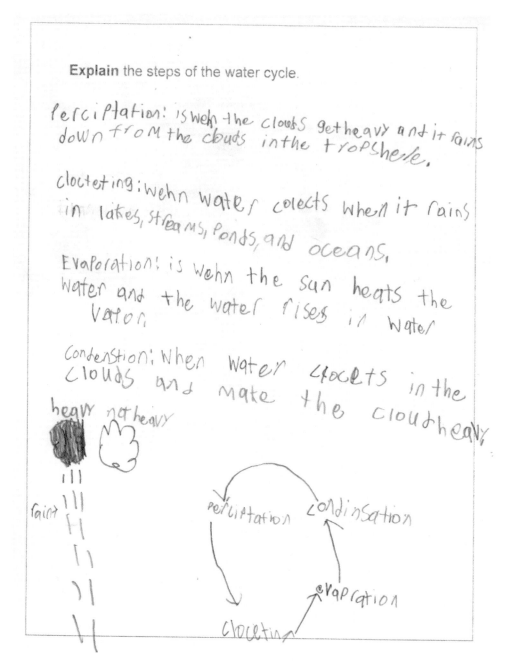

Figure 4.5
Fifth graders review the water cycle in a quick write to prepare for a unit test.

Erin asks students if they feel prepared for the test. Several students admit that they need to review some of the terms or add key details to describe their steps, while others are feeling more confident in their knowledge. Erin is encouraging her students' awareness and sense of agency in their learning with these ten reflective minutes of writing.

Andrea Bretschneider's fifth graders are studying erosion, most recently learning about water's effect on shaping the earth's surface. We have expanded their definition of writing by teaching them to sketchnote—a visual form of note taking. Andrea's students frequently choose to incorporate visual information into their quick writes as well. Today Andrea provides them with a formative quick write they use to describe the three ways water affects the shape of the earth. The sketchnote in Figure 4.6 shows that a student has the basics of erosion and deposition but could use some help clarifying specific details and understanding.

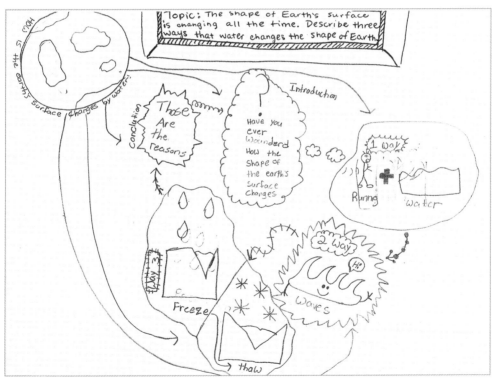

Figure 4.6
Fifth graders use sketchnotes as quick writes.

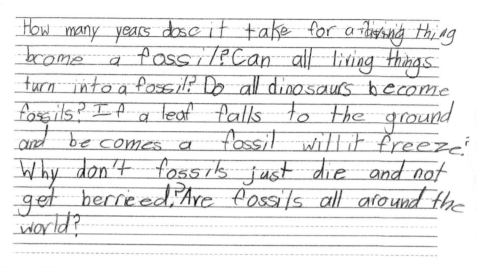

How many years dose it take for a living thing
brome a fossil? Can all living things
turn into a fossil? Do all dinosaurs become
fossils? If a leaf falls to the ground
and becomes a fossil will it freeze?
Why don't fossils just die and not
get berreed? Are fossils all around the
world?

Figure 4.7

Quick writes can spark curiosity before a unit of study.

Caroline Eldridge's second graders are about to embark on a study of fossils. She wants to promote a climate of inquiry, so she uses quick writes to spark their curiosity. Many students want to share what they already know about fossils, but she encourages them to stretch their thinking. She asks them instead, "What do you wonder about fossils?"

Caroline finds the students have some great questions to explore as they learn about fossils. She can also see some misconceptions they have that she will need to address (see Figure 4.7). She tells them this is how scientists start their learning. They wonder. They ask questions. Then they observe, study, and research to discover answers. Sometimes those answers spark even more curiosity.

We often share informational texts and resources with our students that may not link directly to curricular content. It's critical not to limit valuable and interesting information to specific units of study. The same skills and strategies taught during those units can be reinforced with quick writes.

NEWS MAGAZINES FOR VISUALIZING, PREVIEWING, AND PARAPHRASING

Jessica Dejongh's third graders read *Time for Kids* each week. Jessica wants to make the activity more meaningful and the information more memorable for them. We are working on visualizing as well, so we introduce quick writes into the lesson and encourage students to use images as well as words in their responses.

We read an article about the value of artifacts that survived the sinking of the *Titanic* and ask the students what they want to remember about the text. All of them are able to visualize several artifacts to quickly doodle and jot notes before discussing with a partner (see Figure 4.8).

Caroline Eldridge's second graders also read a news magazine every week. Before they read an edition of *Scholastic News*, Caroline invites them to preview the entire magazine and jot down what they are wondering (see Figure 4.9). This quick write activates their schema, familiarizes them with the articles' structure, and cues them into text features such as photos, illustrations, diagrams, and captions. Caroline also notices that this activity

Figure 4.8
Quick writes can incorporate visual and verbal information.

Figure 4.9

A second grader previews weekly news magazine and quick writes what she's wondering.

sparks her students' curiosity and leads to higher levels of engagement as they read the magazine together.

Many teachers often find that when students do research, they have difficulty paraphrasing the information in writing. Jess Walling's fourth graders practice this skill by using a series of quick writes to restate what they read in an informational article. We read a paragraph, then the students take two minutes to paraphrase the big idea. We read the next two paragraphs, and they quick write in the same manner. The writing contains spelling and grammatical errors, but students can put the ideas into their own words quickly and confidently (see Figure 4.10). Breaking down the quick writes by paragraph helps them to see how ideas are clustered together in distinct sections that they can synthesize and summarize. Because each quick write is so short, students process information expeditiously without overthinking or copying. Students should also be taught to credit the source of the information they reference.

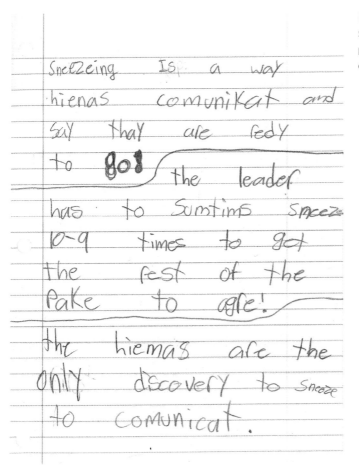

Figure 4.10
Students practice paraphrasing with a series of short quick writes.

Videos for Building Schema

More and more students are learning information through online videos. In 2015, the *Guardian* newspaper reported that YouTube was generating billions of views by kids (Dredge 2015). Ask most students and they can name their favorite YouTubers. The educational videos created by Sal Khan's Khan Academy have proved to be wildly popular for self-paced learning, and sites such as Wonderopolis, TED-Ed, and BrainPOP have also become reliable sources of information for students and teachers. Could quick writes help our students process some of this online learning more purposefully?

BEFORE AND AFTER

Kaitie King's fourth graders are filled with curiosity. They love *Mystery Doug*, a weekly video series that answers science questions asked by real students (https://mysterydoug. com). Most videos are between three and six minutes long and invite students to stop and share their current understanding of the topic before Doug answers a question. Sometimes Kaitie's students turn and talk; other days they quick write their thinking.

Today students are going to discover what the moon is made of. Before they watch the video, Kaitie asks them to take two or three minutes to jot down what they think. Some jokingly write down *cheese*, but most tend to conjecture ambiguously with *rocks*. They watch Doug unravel the mystery and then Kaitie asks them to quick write what they learned and compare it to their original thinking. The length and depth of their responses vary, but all students recognize that they have acquired—and documented—some new scientific learning (see Figures 4.11a and 4.11b).

Figures 4.11a and 4.11b
Fourth graders build schema with quick writes before and after viewing *Mystery Doug* videos.

Infographics

So much of the information we process today is not presented in a narrative form but as infographics—visual presentations of data such as charts and diagrams. When our students quick write responses to infographics, we give them practice in interpreting the data to summarize, synthesize, contemplate purpose, or form opinions. I curated a collection of infographics to inspire quick writes (scan the QR code on this page for access).

 https://bit.ly/2z1gcll

INTERPRETING VISUAL INFORMATION

We display an infographic to Jess Walling's fourth graders. The information compares how many words you would read in a year if you read Harry Potter books for five minutes, twenty minutes, or sixty minutes daily. We ask students to do two short quick writes: first explaining why they think someone created the infographic, then stating what they want to remember from it. Some students even incorporated visual elements into their responses that related to the infographic (see Figure 4.12).

Extracurricular Experiences

Most schools typically schedule field trips, assemblies, presentations, or events that supplement the learning going on in our classrooms. These activities broaden our students' educational experience, but students often aren't given enough time to reflect on them when they happen. Even less frequently do we check in with students down the road to see what still sticks with them. Quick writes don't take a lot of time, but they can encourage students to contemplate personal meaning or wonderings more intentionally.

MAKING CONNECTIONS

Becky Foster's fifth-grade class hosts members of our local Humane Society to give a presentation on the importance of animal population control. Immediately following the presentation, we ask students to respond to the sentence stem "This has me thinking . . ." Their responses remind us that while we often ask students about *what* they learned, it is important to consider the *so what* implications as well. As Figure 4.13 shows, their thinking often goes far beyond the intended lesson.

Infograph Quick Write

I think they made the infograph because they wanted to show us to compare 1hour 20 minutes and 5 minutes every day. And to show if you read twenty minutes a day or a hour or 5 minutes to show how you can tell how much you read every day

1 hour of reading every day

1 hours of reading Harry Potter you read 3,285,000 words.

Harry Potter and the Sorceres Stone

I love reading

Figure 4.12

Fourth graders analyze infographics with a quick write.

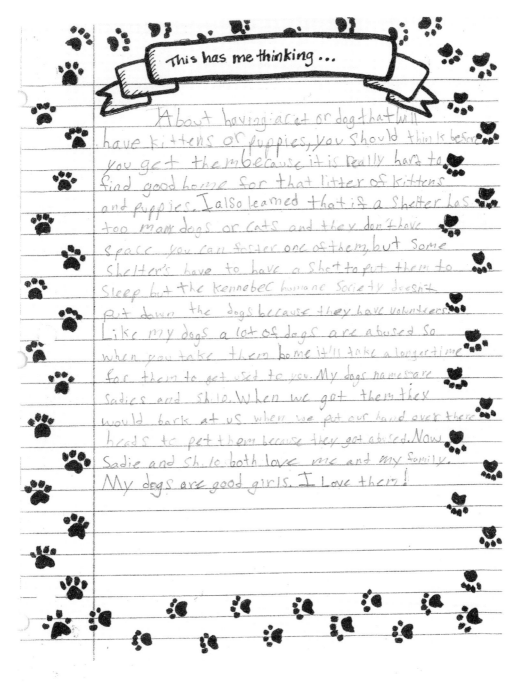

This has me thinking...

About having a cat or dog that will have kittens or puppies, you should think before you get them because it is really hard to find good home for that litter of kittens and puppies. I also learned that if a shelter has too many dogs or cats and they don't have space you can foster one of them, but some shelter's have to have a shot to put them to sleep but the Kennebec humane society doesn't put down the dogs because they have volunteers. Like my dogs a lot of dogs are abused so when you take them home it'll take a longer time for them to get used to you. My dogs names are Sadies and Shilo. When we got them they would bark at us when we put our hand over there heads to pet them because they got abused. Now Sadie and Shilo both love me and my family. My dogs are good girls. I Love them!

Figure 4.13

Quick writes can provide insight into what meaning students take from information.

DETERMINING RELEVANCE

Liz Chadwick's fifth graders have guests from a local credit union come in to speak about an upcoming college scholarship essay contest. Liz and I know the primary goal of the visit is to increase aspirations for all students and give them some rudimentary information about possible careers and college choices, but we are curious about the students' perceptions, so we have them engage in a quick write. Some students give variations of "to learn about college" but others provide more in-depth responses (see Figure 4.14).

QUESTIONING

After a schoolwide assembly combining music, acrobatics, and technology, Caroline Eldridge's second graders are filled with curiosity about how the performers accomplished many of their acts. Rather than ask them what they learned or liked, she taps into their inquisitiveness with a quick write to encourage their sense of wonder (see Figure 4.15). After the students have a chance to jot down their thinking, they engage in a lively conversation that brings to light the similarities and differences in their inquiries and deepens their appreciation of the science embedded in the performance.

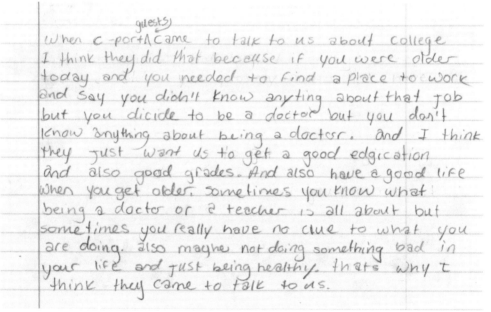

guests)
When c-portA came to talk to us about college I think they did that because if you were older today and you needed to find a place to work and say you didn't know anyting about that job but you dicide to be a doctor but you don't know anything about being a doctor. And I think they just want us to get a good edgication and also good grades. And also have a good life when you get older. Sometimes you know what being a doctor or a teacher is all about but sometimes you really have no clue to what you are doing. Also maybe not doing something bad in your life and just being healthy. thats why I think they came to talk to us.

Figure 4.14

A fifth grader explains the purpose of a guest visitor to the classroom in a quick write.

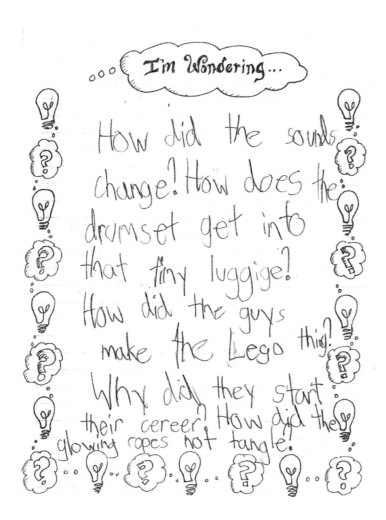

Figure 4.15
Quick writes give
students a chance
to share what they
are wondering after
shared events.

Opinions

Sometimes we have students research a topic and use data or evidence to support a position. This is an important skill to teach our students, but in life we also express personal preferences or beliefs based on our own experiences when we try to persuade others. This type of expression is often driven more by emotion than unbiased information. Too often, we are so invested in our opinions that we aren't open to reflection or discussion—as we see in our polarized society today.

If our students' only experience in forming and expressing opinions is through genre study, they will have limited practice in refining their persuasive-writing skills. More frequent opportunities through quick writes can enhance these skills as well as some critical social-emotional learning. Sharing our personal opinions is only half the task; practicing empathy and understanding for the diverse thinking of others is equally important.

POINT/COUNTERPOINT

Liz Chadwick's fifth graders have been sharing their opinions about a variety of topics with quick writes for the past month. They have become increasingly proficient in getting their ideas down quickly. They enjoy sharing their opinions afterward, but we aren't sure how open they are to the opinions of others. They are polite, but we wonder if they seek to understand or only to express their own thoughts.

Today we give them a piece of paper with two empty boxes. In the first box, we ask them to respond to the statement "It is better to have assigned seats during lunch." They quick write for three minutes. Then in the second box, we ask them to consider who might have a different opinion and why. We want them to contemplate a real person who may hold that opinion—to walk in their shoes to understand why they may not share the same thinking (see Figure 4.16).

The conversations we have this time are much more open and thoughtful. Students talk about their preferences but can see why the lunch monitors, or kids who were excluded and bullied, might want to have assigned seats. They empathize with their reasoning—to feel safe, to have some control, and to keep the lunchroom quieter. We are cultivating understanding and empathy. The more we encourage our kids to see situations or information from multiple perspectives, the more we will develop these critical-thinking skills.

QUESTIONS VS. STATEMENTS

Students rightly see questions as invitations to express their thoughts on a topic. Less frequently are they presented with statements and encouraged to respond them. If we want our children to become wise consumers of information, we want them to know they don't need a formal invitation to contemplate and respond to ideas or claims. We want to encourage a habit of thinking critically about the information they are exposed to in and out of school.

We talk with Liz Chadwick's fifth graders about how claims are often embedded in informational sources. We share a statement based on research at the University of Sheffield that was reported in the *Guardian* newspaper: "The more kids use social media, the less

It is better to have assigned seats during lunch.

I think we should not have assigned seats because if you want to sit with your friends but you couldn't and if you didn't want to sit with the person you were assigned to sit with and because I think everybody should be able to sit with your friends.

I think someone else would have a different opinion because if it was too loud and if someone that was sitting next to you had to move because somebody else was being mean to them or if they could not control it the other people would be sitting in a safe place away from the person that is being mean and not Respectful.

Figure 4.16

Quick writes can help us contemplate alternate perspectives.

happy they feel" (Doward 2017). When several quickly ask if this is true, we ask them whether they would agree or disagree with the claim based on what they know or have experienced. Most tend to agree with it but provide different rationales (see Figure 4.17). We then share the evidence from the article, explaining that the claim is not necessarily true for all kids and that the author is generalizing.

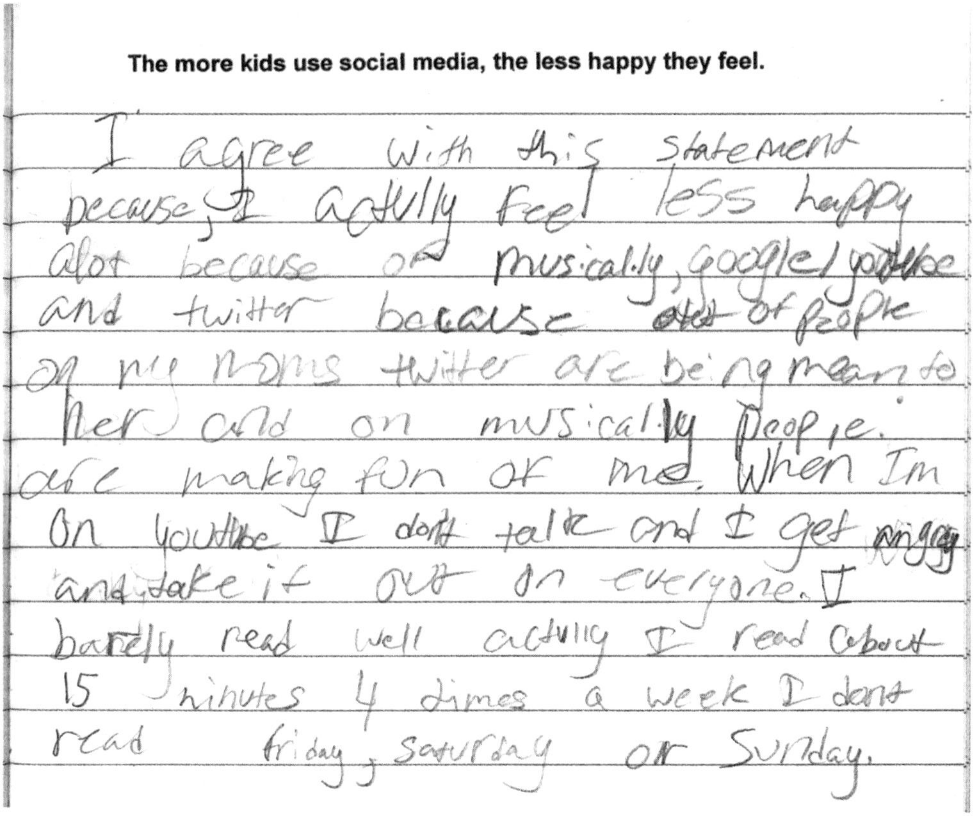

The more kids use social media, the less happy they feel.

> I agree with this statement because, I actully feel less happy alot because of musically, google/youtube and twitter because alot of people on my moms twitter are being mean to her and on musically people are making fun of me. When Im on youtube I dont talk and I get angry and take it out on everyone. I barely read well actully I read about 15 minutes 4 times a week I dont read friday, saturday or Sunday.

Figure 4.17

Quick writing in response to statements, rather than questions, can spark critical thinking.

We are living in a culture inundated with claims and conjecture. If we want our students to successfully navigate these waters, we need to give them plenty of opportunities to practice critical-thinking skills. We can encourage students to find and collect claims and statements in the materials they read or the websites they visit.

PERSUASIVE INFORMATION

Information is presented to our children in so many ways that I can't begin to address every aspect. Much of it lies beyond our classroom walls, but our guidance can help them become more aware of its purpose and effects in their lives. I'm not suggesting it is nefarious material, only that we want our students to make informed judgments about information that is designed to express opinions or persuade.

EDITORIAL CARTOONS

The purpose of editorial cartoons is to creatively express the author's opinion on a topic. They can be difficult for elementary students to comprehend because they often require specific background information and an understanding of satire. I have been curating a collection of editorial cartoons that are accessible to our elementary students and would be a fun stimulus for quick writing. Scan the QR code for access.

 https://bit.ly/2pLPnUZ

I sometimes ask students a very general question to spark their thinking: "What do you think the writer is trying to say?" Responses range from very literal interpretations to personal connections. For example, when I share a cartoon of a "Museum of Extinct Species" showcasing a neighborhood kid who shovels snow, some students interpret it to mean shoveling snow can kill you. Others look for a deeper meaning and begin to understand the satire (Figure 4.18). There's no right response considering the background knowledge this comic requires. Quick writes give students risk-free practice in analyzing visual information and humor as tools of persuasion and encourage deeper thinking in an amusing way.

REVIEWS AND RECOMMENDATIONS

One of the most common ways people share their opinions is through reviews and recommendations. Opinion writing of this sort is a great spark for quick write practice. The more authentic the audience and purpose for the work our students produce, the more likely it is students will carry the skills they learn from it into the world outside of school.

We have done a lot of quick write book reviews in our classrooms. We often choose books that have been recommended by others, so there is an authentic audience readily available for the activity. There may be times when we want more in-depth analysis of books, but quick write reviews are meant to be more casual and improvised. There is also an added element of fun to book selection when you see what others think about titles you are considering.

At a book fair, we provide students with two different slips of paper. One says "Readers will like this book because . . ." (sharing a recommendation). The other says "I'd like to

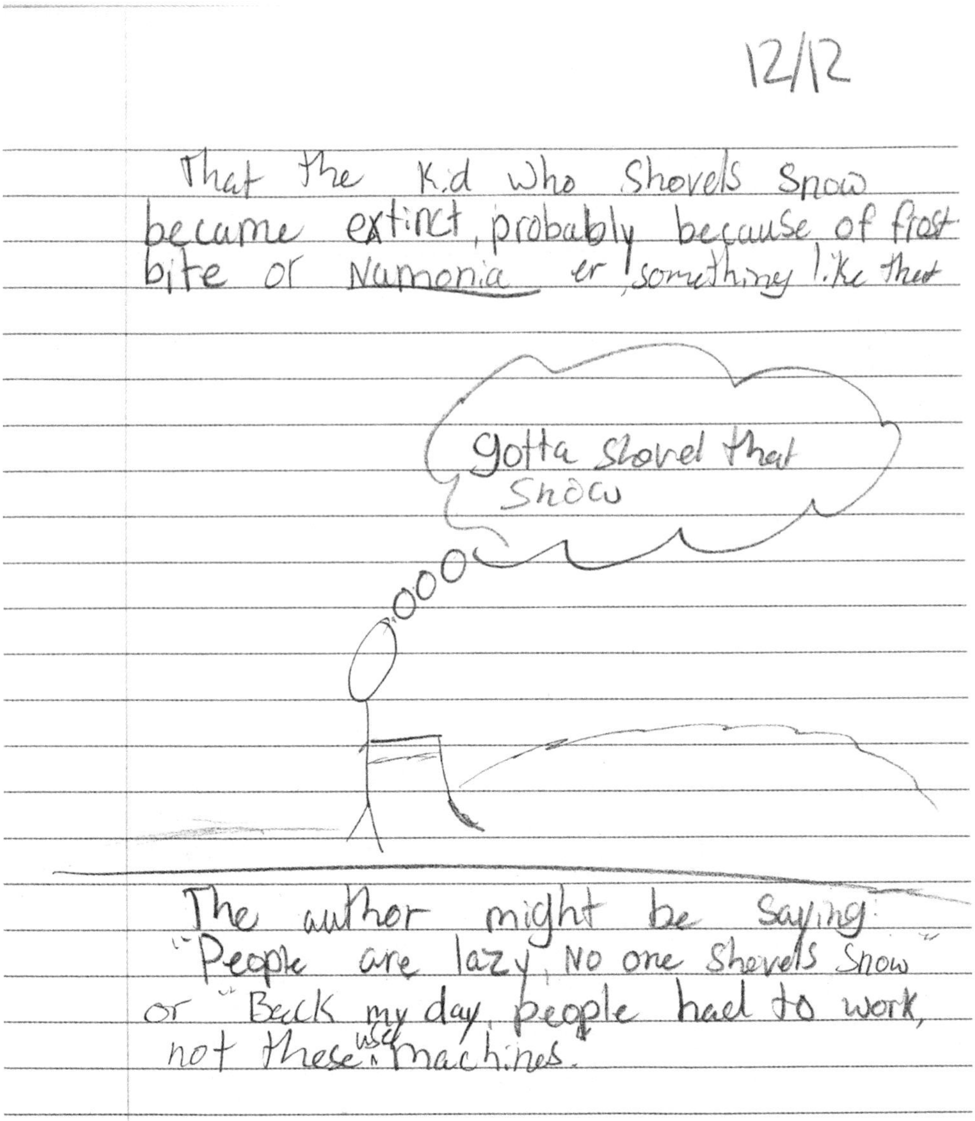

12/12

That the Kid who shovels snow
became extinct, probably because of frost
bite or Numonia er something like that

gotta shovel that
snow

The author might be saying:
"People are lazy, No one shovels snow"
or "Back my day, people had to work,
not these used machines.

Figure 4.18
Fifth graders analyze editorial comics with quick writes.

read _____ because. . ." (reflecting on a previewed book). These slips help parents who attend the fair see what books kids are reading these days and may alert students to books they haven't heard about (see Figure 4.19).

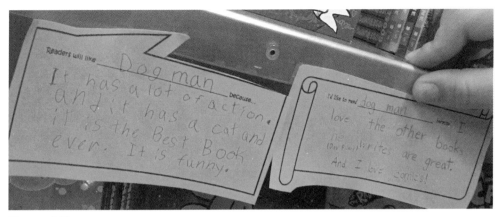

Figure 4.19
Third graders quick write recommendations for a recent book fair.

I frequently observe students browsing for books in our school libraries and becoming entirely overwhelmed by the volume of choices. They often gravitate toward the books with covers facing out—it grabs their attention. So we thought maybe recommendations sticking out of books would grab their attention as well—and it does! We provide students with bookmark-sized slips of paper and invite them to choose a book they've enjoyed to quick write a recommendation or review (see Figure 4.20). We then stick the slip into the book in the library.

There are so many things students could review in a quick write: school lunch offerings, restaurants, favorite snacks, TV shows, movies, YouTube channels. My purpose isn't to share them all but to suggest sparks for your student to use quick writing as a means of expressing their thinking in authentic ways.

Quick Wrap

For our students to grow as writers, they need to write—a lot. They also need to write for a variety of purposes and in diverse modes or genres. Writing across content areas to process learning can be more easily achieved with short and frequent quick writes each day. We want to encourage students to think beyond the *what* of the information they take in and contemplate the *so what*. The physical act of writing stimulates multiple areas of our brains, not only triggering it to pay closer attention but also providing multiple pathways for encoding and retrieving information.

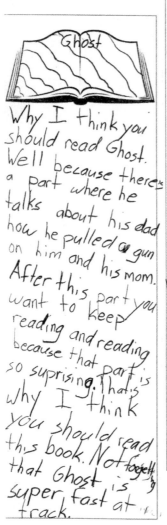

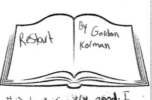

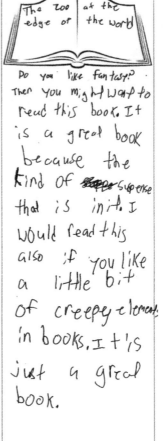

Why I think you should read Ghost. Well because there's a part where he talks about his dad how he pulled a gun on him and his mom. After this part you want to keep reading and reading because that part is so suprising. That is why I think you should read this book. Not forgett that Ghost is super fast at track.

this book is very good. I like it so much because there is just so much to it, like, how chase is trying to make friends, and erase his old history, or how he is part of the video club, or how he doesn't want to play football, even though he was the best player before he hit his head. I love how chase changes so much trougout the book, and I love how realistic it is, I feel like I am using the word "love" alot, but it is the right word to use. You should deffinitly check this book out!

Do you like fantasy? Then you might want to read this book. It is a great book because the kind of suspense that is in it. I would read this also if you like a little bit of creepy elements in books. It's just a great book.

Figure 4.20

Quick write reviews get tucked into books to entice potential readers.

We also form opinions based on the information we process and the experiences we encounter. Building our awareness of the diversity of opinions shaped by interpreting information and the experiences of others is an effective way to promote empathy and understanding.

Quick Write Invite

How do your students typically respond to information they consume?

What types of critical thinking would you most like to encourage?

CHAPTER 5

Appreciation Quick Writes: Bringing the Arts Back to Language Arts

APPRECIATION QUICK WRITES

Why do we call it language **ARTs** if we don't help our students appreciate the aesthetics of reading and writing? What about visual literacy? We live in such a visual world – I want our students to think more critically in it. They need opportunities and practice to notice and respond – to process their experience. Many believe art is what makes us human – fine arts, performing arts, language arts. Let's explore these – and our humanity through writing!

Figure 5.1

My quick write

QUICK GLANCE: Appreciation quick writes spark students' appreciation for the art that celebrates our humanity to cultivate more meaningful lives.

Language Arts

It's called language arts for a reason. I believe that reading, writing, listening, speaking, and viewing are arts because the aesthetics and personal meaning that we bring to those tasks can enrich our lives, inspire creativity, and document our human experience. If we teach these tasks with a singular goal of proficient skill acquisition and not with a goal of developing an appreciation of the language arts, we might want to rename the subject *language science.* I believe we need to embrace the artistry of our language study and build connections to the fine arts for our students to realize their full potential not only as learners but also as human beings.

This chapter offers quick write lessons that encourage students to engage with a variety of art in visual, auditory, or verbal formats. This combination of formats activates multiple areas of the brain to spark students' thinking and processing of information. These quick writes are intended to encourage students to notice, wonder, and appreciate the world around them through the arts while increasing volume, stamina, and skill with writing.

Why Appreciation Is Important

In a 2013 blog post, Rachel Naomi Remen wrote: "Most of us lead far more meaningful lives than we know. Often finding meaning is not about doing things differently; it is about seeing familiar things in new ways" (Remen 2013). As a teacher and a parent, I believe there is nothing more important than helping our children lead meaningful lives. Too often I see people sleepwalk through life, taking so many things for granted. They have little gratitude for the everyday wonders and joys around them. I want our students to cultivate an awareness of the arts, the nature, the people, and the world around them. I want them to build a practice of appreciation that will enhance their physical and emotional well-being. I want them to recognize that there are many ways to respond to experiences and that they have agency in interpreting these experiences.

Appreciation can happen only when we tune in, notice, and become more aware. We can't always take our students out into the world to do this, so we can look for ways to bring the world into our classrooms. We can share photos, videos, art, stories, music, or poetry that reflect the human experience and invite students to notice and respond through writing. These quick writes can be the spark to help our students walk more fully present through their lives. Because this writing isn't tied to a curriculum or workshop study, we are free to experiment with wide-ranging options and expose students to an eclectic assortment of artistic forms. I know that as I've collected and shared these resources with my students, my own appreciation of the arts and humanities has increased considerably.

Photos

I often start this quick write approach with photographs because they are so ubiquitous in our lives. Photos may be purposefully composed or randomly captured. Photos freeze moments in time that allow us to attend to detail and notice what we might otherwise overlook. They invite us to contemplate a story, to imagine a context, to consider a perspective. Quick writes with photos can help our students see something familiar in new ways by taking the time to look and think with intention.

The "visual to verbal" process of thinking and writing about photos activates multiple areas of the brain and allows for broad interpretation and creativity. An uncaptioned photo enables a writer to invent a meaning and take off in a wide variety of directions. Some writers may describe what they see. Others may create a narrative or a poem inspired by the image. Still others may find forgotten memories awakened. All these responses encourage our students to notice more purposefully.

Jessica Walling's fourth graders love the fact that I take most of the photographs we use for quick writes. They are intrigued by the stories behind the pictures, and we encourage them to channel that sense of wonder into their quick writes. We project a photo onto the whiteboard and invite students to tell a story, share a memory, create a poem, describe what they see—how they respond is entirely their choice. Jessica and I are fascinated by how varied their thinking, styles, or approaches can be. We see them growing in their appreciation for photography as well as storytelling (see Figures 5.2a and 5.2b).

MYSTERY PHOTOS

Co-creating classroom resources with students provides them with a sense of agency and ownership in the learning and encourages another layer of mindfulness in the process. Andrea Bretschneider's fifth grade students take turns sharing a "mystery photo" with their classmates. With an instant camera, she assigns them the task of photographing something in the school that could spark their classmates to respond in writing. This task

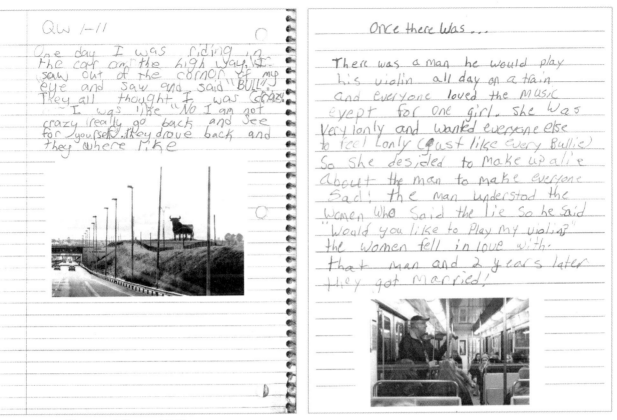

QW 1-11

One day I was riding in the car on the high way, I saw out of the cornor of my eye and saw and said "BULL" They all thought I was crazy. I was like "No I am not crazy (really go back and see for yourself. They drove back and they where like

Once there was...

There was a man he would play his violin all day on a train and everyone loved the music eyept for one girl. she was very lonly and wanted everyone else to feel Lonly (Just like every Bullie) So she desided to make up a lie about the man to make everyone sad! the man understod the women who said the lie so he said "would you like to play my violin?" the women fell in love with that man and 2 years later they got married!

Figures 5.2a and 5.2b
Fourth graders quick write narratives from a photo.

encourages them to look at their environment with greater awareness and appreciation. We love to see what they choose, as well as how they frame the image. We then collect the snapshots to use as mystery photos for quick writes (see Figure 5.3).

Andrea's class assembles photo books out of their quick writes. This class anthology (see Figure 5.4) gives her students an authentic audience for writing and helps them appreciate the diversity of ideas that can come from a single image. We also invite students to bring photos from home, to help build home/school connections and create more personalized learning.

Quick write
Mystery Picture

*Use your classmate's picture
to start a story.*

"What a lovely park" Kailey said,
"Yay" Suri replied back maybe we should go for
a walk by the pound. Kailey and Suri wacthed
the fish swim in the pound as the day
turned darker and the sun was setting.
Whoosh a falcon picked up a fish and started
going directly to Kaileys face.
"lookout" Suri screamd. Kailey looked
at the falcon the falcon looked at her and
then...
"ahhh" Kailey screamd, then she quickly duck
and turned around The falcon was heading
for her agin she ducked and the falcon
hit a park tree and started flying up in to the
sky.
"good job ducking" Suri said
"Well it was more of a duck to save my life" said Kailey
And then they both laughed.

Figure 5.3
Students quick write stories from photos taken by peers.

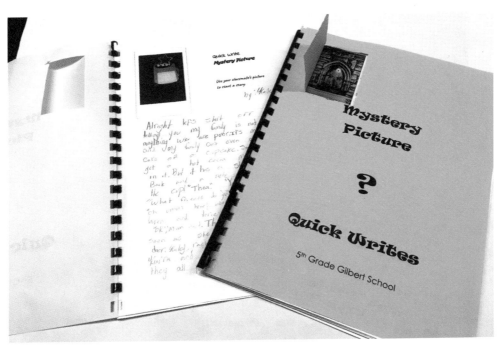

Figure 5.4
An anthology of quick writes celebrates the diversity of thinking.

Here are some photo collection ideas:

- Teacher-curated photo albums. Taking photos to inspire stories helps us to be more observant as we walk through this world and to personalize our lessons for students. Children are curious about their teachers' lives, and our photos can bring pieces of us into the classroom. Scan the QR code to access a Google Photo album I've created with photographs I have taken over the past few years.

https://bit.ly/2ONLVaq

- Free image collections. While you can find a plethora of photos and images online with a simple search, be sure the ones you choose are not subject to copyright laws by looking for ones licensed as "Creative Commons" (i.e., free to use). You can bookmark websites or create your own collection. I used Padlet to create a virtual bulletin board of copyright-free photos; scan the QR code for access.

 https://bit.ly/2ysX6LC

- Student photo collections. Inviting students to bring in photos from their lives outside school increases awareness and appreciation and provides insights into our students' lives.

FINDING FREE IMAGES ON GOOGLE

1. Enter your search term, and click "Images" below the search box.

2. Click "Settings," and choose "Advanced Search" from the drop-down menu.

3. Scroll down to the "Usage Rights" drop-down menu, and select "free to use or share."

You may also select "Safe Search" to filter any explicit results.

Art

"Wait. That's art?" a sixth grader giggles as I share a Jackson Pollock painting. Indeed, art *is* in the eye of the beholder, often ambiguous and open to interpretation. It can encourage new ways of thinking or expressing the human experience. People rarely look at art and have no reaction, so it is a powerful spark for inviting responses. In fact, there is a growing and fascinating field of neuroaesthetics examining just how the brain processes a work of art. For example, Harvard professor Nancy L. Etcoff studies how "art arouses an extremely complex whole-brain response that brings into play many usually disparate aspects of the mind." She describes it as "mind wandering and involves thoughts about the self, memory, and future" (quoted in Pak and Reichsman 2017). We can tap into this mind-wandering energy with quick writes.

We don't ask students to interpret or evaluate art; we encourage mindful responses. Some may write a description, interpretation, or evaluation of the art itself, while others might react with emotion, memories, or personal connections. They may notice preferences, look more purposefully, or develop a greater appreciation of art while flexing their writing muscles each day. I have often found that the more interesting the art, the more interesting the responses!

I share my Padlet of artworks with Guy Meader's sixth-grade students. This collection represents a wide range of art movements: from Realism to Surrealism, Impressionism to Abstract Expressionism. I try to make sure my own preferences do not bias my selections, but there is so much art in the world with which I am not yet familiar. For a week, Guy's students select a piece of art each day that catches their attention and write for five minutes about it. We can offer some prompts to get started, but we tell them there is no *right way* to respond (see Figures 5.5a and 5.5b).

Storm in the Rockies
Albert Bierstadt

In the painting I choose - *Storm in the Rockies* I looked at the different colors drifting next to the tall mountains. In the back there's a mountain, it glistens with golden reflecting off the sun. It's the only mountain tall enough to be seen above the clouds. Tree's have fallen hoping to not fall the tremendous drop, their leaves still green but falling from the oak wood. I'm thinking about the storm and where it's going. I'm feeling like I want to hike those mountains. To look down from the top and see what I've accomplished. Happy to try something new and have succeeded at it, looking down on what I used to thought was a painting but no, nothing could ever capture this beauty and this feeling.

The scream
Edvard Munch

i think that this means that it's going to be the end of the world sooner than you think like it's screaming because of an asteroid going to hit earth and the other people in the back are taking picture of it when they are about to die or judging from how it looks maybe it's about the pollution in the ocean because it looks like there's oil in the water and it looks like there's boats that are spreading the oil

Figures 5.5a and 5.5b
Sixth graders respond to art work with quick writes.

A simple Internet search by artist, art movement and styles, or medium will give you thousands of images to choose from. I've pulled together a small collection of art to get you started. (Scan the QR code for access.)

https://bit.ly/2pOBc17

Here are some sparks to use with art quick writes:

- What are you thinking?
- What are you feeling?
- What do you notice?
- What do you wonder?

EKPHRASIS

Want to impress students with an artistic form of writing that has been around for centuries? Teach them about ekphrastic writing. This form of prose or poetry is inspired or stimulated by a work of art; the goal is to make the reader envision the art described as if it were physically present. The word *ekphrastic* is an Ancient Greek term meaning "description." A good mentor text for this type of writing is *World Make Way: New Poems Inspired by Art from the Metropolitan Museum of Art*, edited by Lee Bennett Hopkins (2018).

Kaitie King's fourth graders recently select one of four paintings about which to quick write vivid descriptions, and when they share, their peers try to determine which piece they are describing. This activity encourages students to look carefully at the art pieces as they write as well as to listen closely to the ekphrastic writing of their peers. One student shares she can't wait to go home and teach her parents about ekphrasis. Use the QR code to see if you can determine which painting students chose for the ekphrastic quick writes in Figures 5.6a and 5.6b.

https://bit.ly/2w4DSMY

"A face so colorful
and bright A part
filled with only
black and white
long beautiful eyel-
ashes and a pretty
hat where only one
tear stands"

2.

different shapes
all different
colors where
only a small part
of black and
white
stand

3.

Green, yellow, red, and
blue with a touch of
white and some
black oh look purple
too

Weird Man

Girl or Boy
look like eating
paper Gross earring
Big Eya Drows stars
in Eyas Big Eya lashes
Pretty Green hands
(probly did int was themsbraactx)
long Blue hair nice Blake
Cought Red hat yellow exsosry
Blue flower yellow walls
Little Bit of Blue andred
ears smosher By earing or
a Ring I Dont know Red
towers lots of red and
Blue yellow skin to
toy Dont tool he must
have never wash his
self you can kinda see
it Bones

Figures 5.6a and 5.6b
Can you guess which famous painting these fourth graders composed
ekphrastic quick writes about?

Music

Music is created by combining elements to form a composition. Writing is a fundamentally similar process. Both can tell a story, stir our emotions, and shape experience. Music speaks to us on so many levels—emotionally, socially, intellectually, and spiritually. It is so pervasive that we often don't notice or appreciate it consciously, but it certainly has an impact on emotions and interpretation of experiences.

I am working with Liz Chadwick's fifth grade students on quick writes this year. I select a piece of instrumental music and watch as they mindfully listen before responding. They tune into their emotions, memories, and visualizations evoked by the composition to quick write in a variety of ways. As students later share, there are often murmurs of, "Same!" or "Oh, yeah!" in response to their peers' writing.

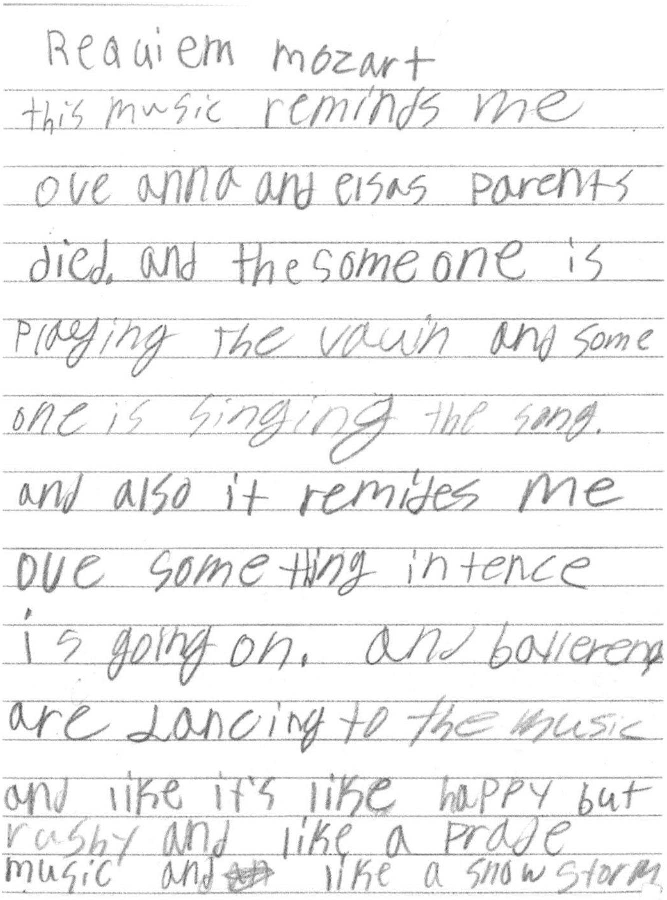

> Reauiem mozart
> this music reminds me
> ove anna and elsas parents
> died. and thesomeone is
> plauing the vauin and some
> one is singing the song.
> and also it remiges me
> ove something intence
> is going on. and ballerena
> are Lancing to the music
> and like it's like happy but
> rushy and like a prage
> music and like a snow storm

Figure 5.7

Quick write response to Mozart's "Requiem"

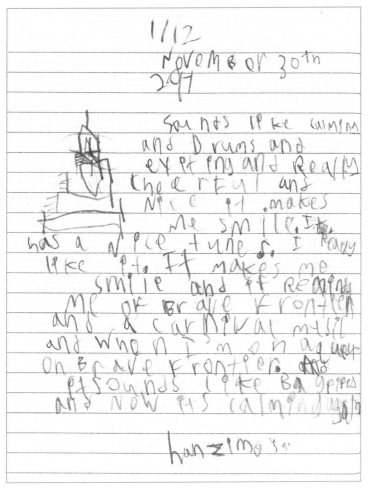

Figure 5.8
Quick write response to *The Last of the Mohicans* soundtrack

Liz's students have commented that they are more aware of the music that surrounds them after engaging in these quick writes. They notice the soundtrack music on TV or in movies and talk about how it makes them feel during the different scenes. I was stunned when several students' writing matched the intended themes of an unidentified composer's work. One girl responds to Mozart's "Requiem" (Figure 5.7) and another to *The Last of the Mohicans* soundtrack ("The Gael" by Dougie MacLean) (Figure 5.8) without knowing the title or composer until afterward. Their astute responses floor me. Clearly these students are beginning to tune in and appreciate the aesthetics of music more keenly.

You can find many classical works of music online if you don't already own them. I've collected a Padlet of varied music—from classics to modern instrumentals to soundtracks—that can help you get started (scan the QR code).

https://bit.ly/2ypMywC

Although we have primarily focused on instrumental music because the meaning isn't already laid out through lyrics, I think using pop music can also spark writing ideas.

SONG LYRICS

Song lyrics are not typically a part of the canon of literature in most elementary classrooms, but they could be. Lyrics are meant to be shared in the context of a musical backdrop, but strip the melody and rhythm away and they are indistinguishable from poetry. Like poets, songwriters choose words and phrases to purposefully convey ideas and emotions. This is indeed a way of seeing something familiar in new ways to find deeper meaning.

Guy Meader's sixth graders are quick writing in Google Classroom. They choose a song's lyrics from a collection I created on a Padlet (scan QR code) and linked to their quick write assignment tab. They are invited to "Choose a line or a phrase from this song lyric. What does it make you think of? Feel? Remember? Imagine?" Some students choose the same song but find different lines that speak to them—they have very different responses (see Figure 5.9).

https://bit.ly/2pNKO7H

Song Lyrics Quick Writes

Humble and Kind sung by Tim McGraw Lyrics by Lori McKenna

Don't take for granted the love this life gives you

    This line speaks to me because any day someone could die. You will never get to say I love you or sorry, ever again. So when you are about to do something stupid think about it and think about how you would feel about never getting to talk to them again. Make sure that you live with compassion and loyalty to everyone because today could be your last.

Humble and Kind sung by Tim McGraw Lyrics by Lori McKenna

When it's hot, eat a root beer popsicle

This line speaks to me because, usually every summer I always have a popsicle when it's a hot summer day. I don't think I ever had a root beer popsicle I think I had a chocolate popsicle. You know it sounds weird but it taste so good. I like this line because it shows how when it's hot jus have a popsicle and cool down, this speaks to me as if I were on a beach.

Believer by Imagine Dragons

I'ma say all the words inside my head
So the first line I can connect with is because, If I think something I will say it. I may ask myself if I should, but even if I do I still say it. I am a very blunt person. So if someone is being mean to me I will say that they are being rude, and tell them what I think of that. I won't be rude to them but I'll tell them What I think.
I'm the one at the sail, I'm the master of my sea, oh-ooh
    So the second line I connect with because sometimes I can be really bossy and rude. So I think of myself as a leader. Or that they will do what I say...

Believer by Imagine Dragons

I was broken from a young age

I don't really know why this speaks to me, but it does. I am just sad a lot, and it is really annoying, and it started when I was like 7 or so. And i don't really have anyone to talk to other than ▮ so...

Figure 5.9
Sixth graders choose lines from song lyrics to respond with a quick write.

One challenge for elementary teachers attempting to collect song lyrics from our popular culture is the appropriateness of language and content for this age group. More than once I've thought a song's lyrics were suitable until they were written down on a page and I could analyze them more carefully. You might want to consult urbandictionary.com to see if a lyricist has woven double entendres into a seemingly innocuous song. I've started a collection of lyrics that are kid-friendly on my Padlet, but use your discretion. You know your kids and the appropriateness for your school situation.

Poetry

Linda Rief and Penny Kittle are my mentors when it comes to quick writes on poetry. When I listen to them talk about their middle and high school students writing daily to poems with heartfelt honesty or joyous humor, I know our elementary students can respond as well. Because many poems are short, they can convey compelling ideas and feelings with a few well-chosen words or phrases and can be digested more quickly than most prose, making them ideal for quick writes.

In Liz Chadwick's fifth grade class, students share poems from Amy Ludwig VanDerwater's website The Poem Farm (http://www.poemfarm.amylv.com/). Each student receives a copy of the poems we read. They can think about ideas or themes of the entire poem or lift a word or line that speaks to them and respond however they like (see Figure 5.10).

Some kids write straightforward interpretations that started with "I think this poem is about . . ." Others are more playful and creative in their responses, but all are personal and meaningful. The more these kids experience connecting with poems and hearing the responses of others, the greater their appreciation for poetry grows.

Literature

Reading journals and logs can be found in most elementary classrooms and book bags. You can find hundreds of reader response ideas with a Google search or on Pinterest. Before building a stockpile of reading prompts, I encourage you to think carefully about the purpose behind the quick writes. If you use writing as an accountability tool to make sure students are reading independently, I beg you to reconsider. Anecdotal evidence and research have shown that "students with mandatory logs expressed declines in both interest and attitudes towards recreational reading" (Pak and Weseley 2012). We want quick writes to enhance our students' enjoyment and appreciation for the arts and literature,

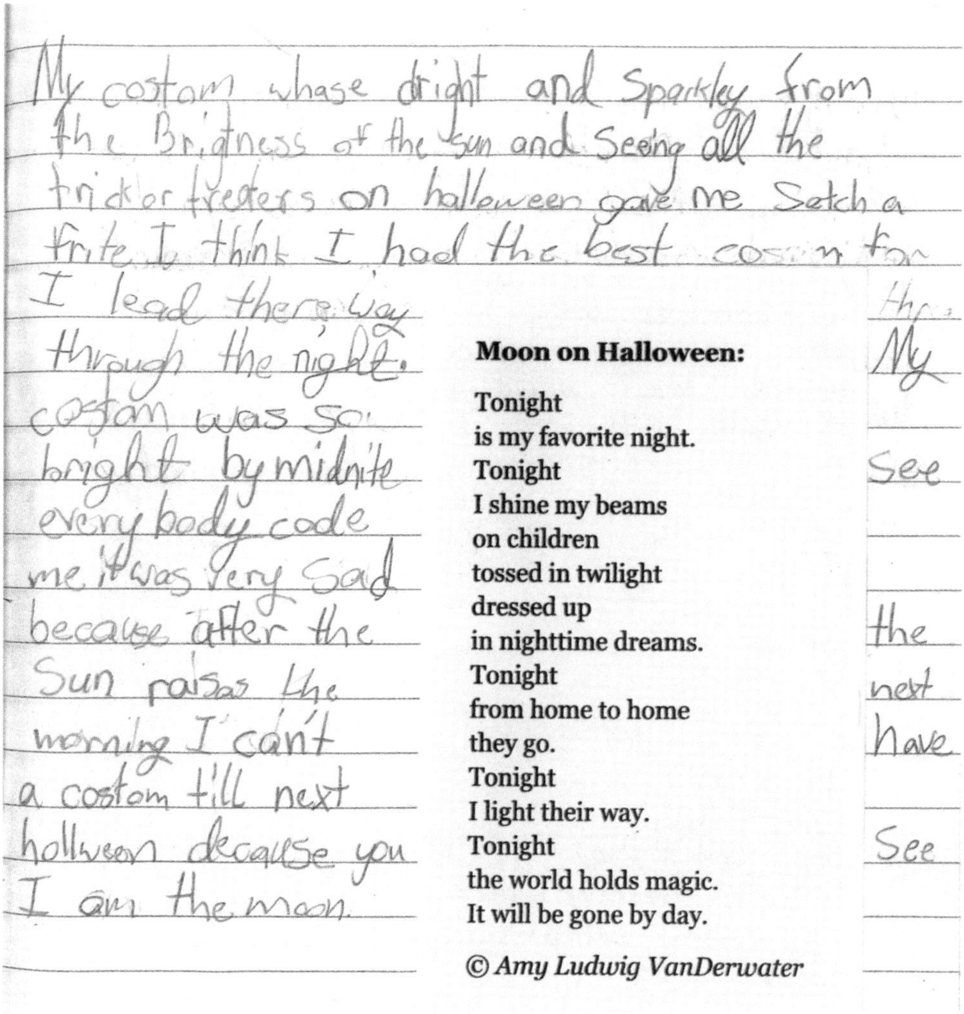

My costom whase bright and sparkley from the brigness of the sun and seeing all the trick or treaters on halloween gave me setch a frite. I think I had the best cosmn for I lead there way through the night. My costom was so bright by midnite everybody code me it was very sad because after the sun raises the morning I can't a costom till next hollween because you I am the moon.

Moon on Halloween:

Tonight
is my favorite night.
Tonight
I shine my beams
on children
tossed in twilight
dressed up
in nighttime dreams.
Tonight
from home to home
they go.
Tonight
I light their way.
Tonight
the world holds magic.
It will be gone by day.

© *Amy Ludwig VanDerwater*

Figure 5.10
Fifth grader quick writes to Amy Ludwig VanDerwater's "Moon on Halloween"

not diminish it.

I propose using quick writes to spark readers' thinking and appreciation for the work of the author. I observe in Samantha Simmons's fourth-grade classroom as she pauses during a read-aloud of *Wonder* by R.J. Palacio and repeats a sentence she just read: "Always try to be a little kinder than is necessary." She lets the words hang in the air a moment before inviting her students to quick write about what the quote brings to mind (see Figure 5.11).

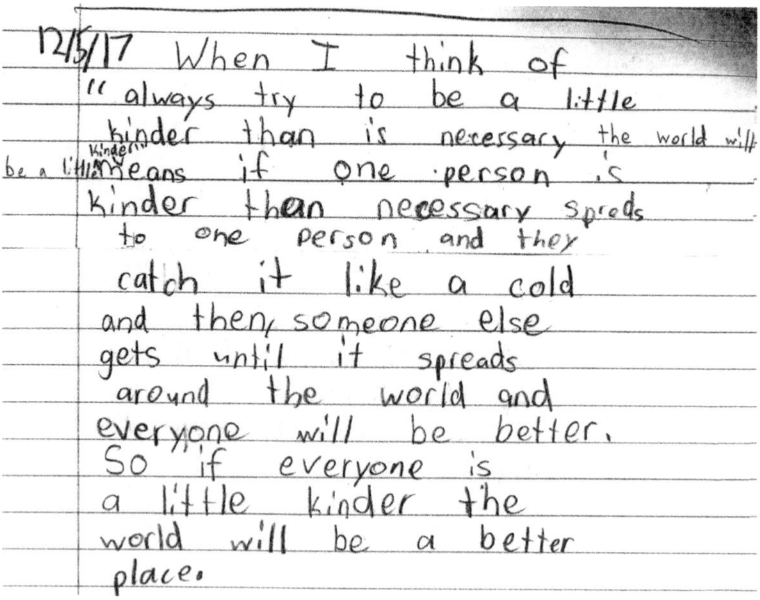

12/5/17 When I think of "always try to be a little kinder than is necessary the world will be a little" means if one person is kinder than necessary spreds to one person and they catch it like a cold and then, someone else gets until it spreads around the world and everyone will be better. So if everyone is a little kinder the world will be a better place.

Figure 5.11

A fourth grader responds to a line from R. J. Palacio's *Wonder.*

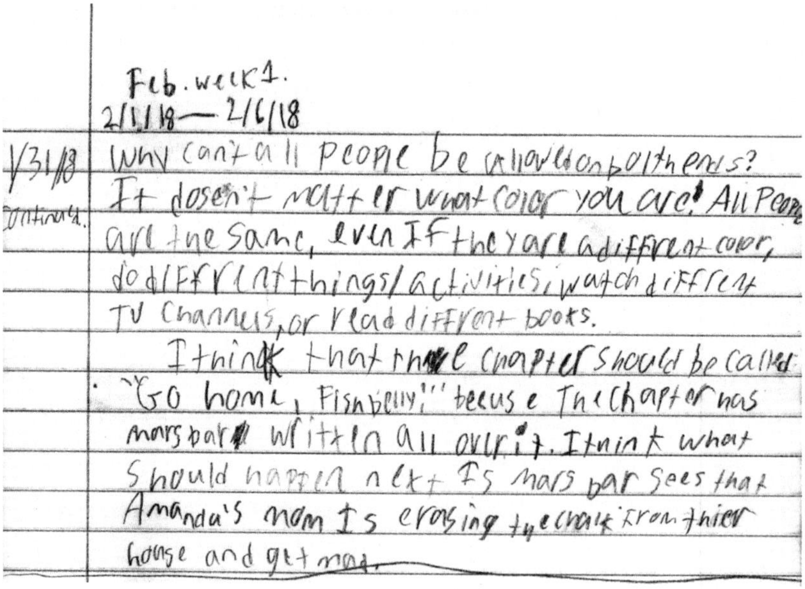

Feb. week 4.
2/1/18 — 2/6/18

1/31/18
continued.

Why can't all people be unworldsonpolthenes? It dosen't matter what color you are! All People are the same, even If they are a different color, do different things/activities, watch different TV Channels, or read different books.

I think that this chapter should be called "Go home, Fishbelly," becuse the chapter has mars bar written all over it. I think what should happen next is mars bar sees that Amanda's mom is erosing the chalk from thier house and get mad.

Figure 5.12

Fourth graders create chapter titles as quick writes for Jerry Spinelli's *Maniac Magee.*

Not only do the students respond quickly and enthusiastically to Samantha's selected phrases, they now stop her and suggest lines they consider "quick write worthy"! They frequently highlight a sentence or phrase in their own reading to share with Samantha when they believe it deserves notice and reflection. This is the epitome of appreciation.

Later, while reading *Maniac Magee* by Jerry Spinelli, Samantha asks the students to come up with their own chapter titles and explain their choices. Students are unpacking themes, determining importance, and synthesizing information as they consider possible titles for each chapter (see Figure 5.12). At a glance, Samantha can see the meaning students are taking from the text and making their own. The students notice and appreciate the decisions authors make when crafting a title for an entire book as well as for individual chapters.

Daily quick writes can remind readers they are active participants in constructing meaning with the author. Giving students an opportunity to share their quick writes helps them appreciate how each reader may come away from the same text with different ideas, especially if the prompts are open-ended. This can be incredibly empowering, particularly for students who worry more about getting the right answer rather than understanding, appreciating, and enjoying the books they read (and the authors who write them).

Wordless Books

What better way to explore art and literature than delving into wordless picture books? These offer exquisite opportunities for quick writes that let students consider what is happening through their own individual lenses.

Kaitie King's fourth-grade students are using Chris Van Allsburg's classic book *The Mysteries of Harris Burdick*—which is nearly wordless—as a spark for quick writes. Some students' writing reflects noticing and wondering, as with the ekphrastic quick writes; others embrace a more creative approach to storytelling and bring the illustration to life (see Figure 5.13).

Book Trailers

Book trailers are intended as video advertisements for books, but I also see them as an art form. Trailers visually entice readers to consider titles they may not have otherwise. Many have an emotional element interwoven, with a musical score or other cinematic film techniques that capture the imagination. We can use trailers to activate student thinking

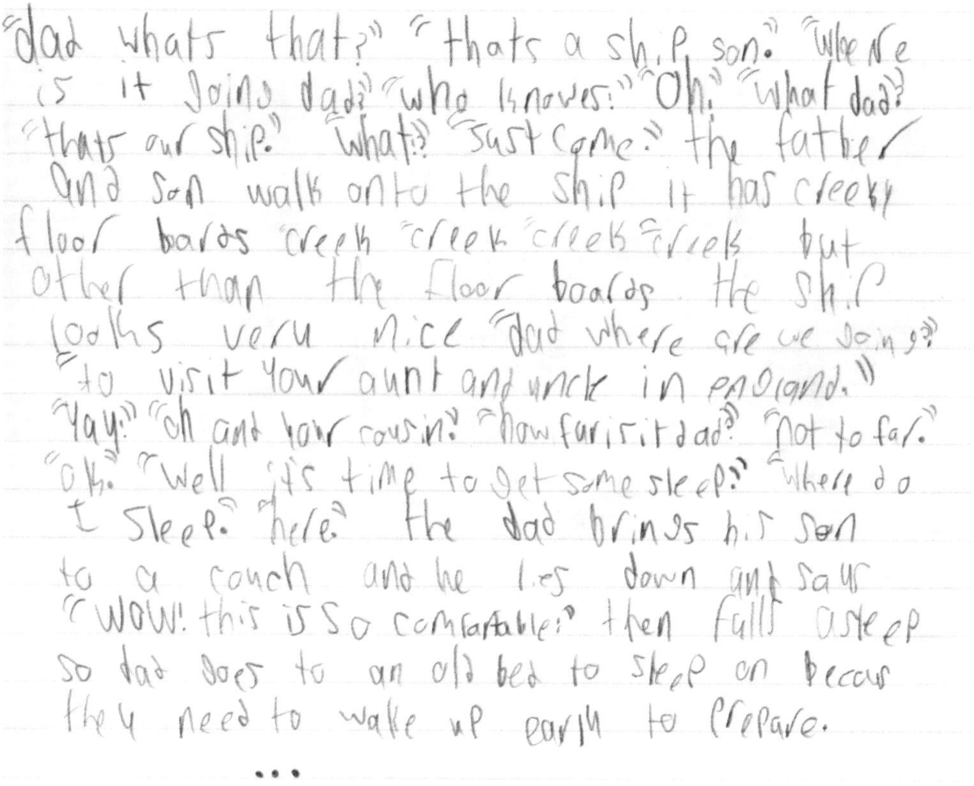

"dad whats that?" "thats a ship son." "where
is it going dad?" "who knows." "Oh." "what dad?
"thats our ship." "what?" "Just come." the father
and son walk onto the ship it has creeky
floor bards creek creek creek creek but
other than the floor boards the ship
looks very nice "dad where are we going?"
"to visit your aunt and uncle in england."
"Yay" "oh and your cousin." "how far is it dad?" "not to far."
"ok." "well its time to get some sleep?" "where do
I sleep?" "here" the dad brings his son
to a couch and he lies down and says
"wow! this is so comfortable." then falls asleep
so dad goes to an old bed to sleep on becaus
they need to wake up early to prepare.

· · ·

Figure 5.13
Wordless books are great sparks for quick write responses.

before they hold a text in their hands. Quick writes in response to viewing a trailer can give students a chance to ponder, consider, or evaluate potential future reads.

Before winter break, Liz Chadwick shares several book trailers with her students to pique their interest for vacation reading. Then she asks them to quick write about what books interest them and why. *Refugee* by Alan Gratz caught the attention of many students (see Figure 5.14). This quick write activity also works well for opinion writing (see Chapter 4) if you encourage students to create reviews or share recommendations of books based on the trailer.

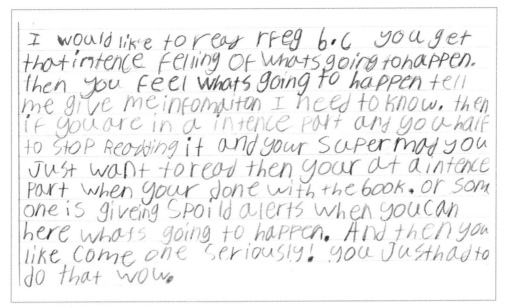

Figure 5.14

A fifth grader responds to the book trailer for Alan Gratz's *Refugee.*

I've created Padlets for middle-grade and picture-book trailers to help you get started (scan the QR codes). Consider what genres, titles, and authors could help expand your students' appreciation for a variety of literature.

https://bit.ly/2Psk4cO
Middle grade book trailers

https://bit.ly/2pMRYxJ
Picture book trailers

Quick Wrap

Art exists in every culture, country, and community. It reflects and communicates human experience in a way that is accessible and enjoyable to almost everyone. It can help us achieve better self-awareness when we take the time to notice, explore, or interpret what we are experiencing and feeling. Interactions with art activate different regions of our brain to process information. Writing about what we see, hear, and feel helps these regions to interact more effectively.

Neuroscientists contend that "intelligence depends on the brain's ability to integrate information from verbal, visual, spatial and executive processes" (Barbey et al. 2012). Five to ten minutes of quick writing could be the boost our students need to increase their intelligence as well as their appreciation for the world around them. Maybe it's time we bring more arts back into our language arts!

Quick Write Invite

How could incorporating more arts into language arts benefit your students?

Which arts would they respond to best?

CHAPTER 6

Creativity Quick Writes: Composing and Communicating

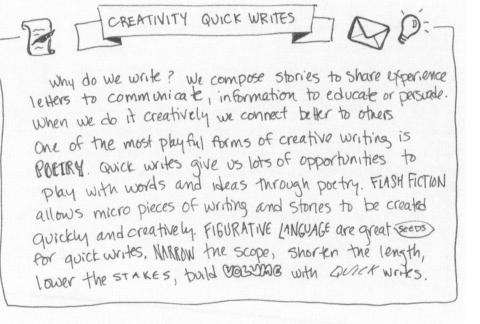

CREATIVITY QUICK WRITES

why do we write? We compose stories to share experience letters to communicate, information to educate or persuade. When we do it creatively we connect better to others

One of the most playful forms of creative writing is POETRY. Quick writes give us lots of opportunities to play with words and ideas through poetry. FLASH FICTION allows micro pieces of writing and stories to be created quickly and creatively. FIGURATIVE LANGUAGE are great SEEDS for quick writes. NARROW the scope, shorten the length, lower the STAKES, build VOLUME with QUICK writes.

Figure 6.1
My quick write

QUICK GLANCE: Quick writes for composing and communicating invite students to play with words and language to spark creative thinking in a low-stakes environment.

The quick writes in this chapter may resemble minilessons that you encourage students to try out in writers' notebooks or as part of a unit of study because they are focused on composing. However, the purpose isn't to tie these small bursts of writing to your current workshop focus. These quick writes are great to use when students are immersed in expository, research, or argument units of study, allowing them to dip their toes back into narrative waters as a refresher. They will invite poetry into our students' lives beyond National Poetry Month or a genre study, making it as familiar and commonplace as prose.

Composition

Composing often refers to the creation of work by combining elements. Just as musicians combine rhythm, harmony, and melody and visual artists combine line, shape, and color, writers use ideas, organization, and word choice (among other elements). It is important to note that composers aren't creating something out of nothing—they use what they know to inspire their compositions.

Creativity quick writes give students opportunities to play with a variety of familiar elements to compose short pieces of writing. By isolating components that promote creativity or enhance communication and by giving students multiple opportunities for playful practice, we can help them develop writing skills more proficiently with purposeful attention.

Aristotle once said, "It is frequent repetition that produces a natural tendency." Repeated practice is a cornerstone for learning. Tasks can become second nature as skills transfer from the conscious to the subconscious. The barriers to writing that students create (indecision, lack of confidence, resistance) can be worn away with daily quick writes that are engaging and creative. Let's look at those aspects of creativity and communication that we can practice.

Creativity

I have too often heard the lament, "We don't have time for creativity anymore; we need to teach these standards." As teachers, we feel pressure to maximize instructional time. If we have a definition of creativity that narrowly focuses on being "artsy," we may feel inadequate or expect specialist teachers to cover it. Consider Robert Franken's definition instead: "Creativity is defined as the tendency to generate or recognize ideas, alternatives, or possibilities that may be useful in solving problems, communicating with others, and entertaining ourselves and others" (Franken 1994, 396). We all want our students to solve problems, communicate with others, and enjoy learning. Quick writes provide a spark to explore ideas and build a creative daily practice.

Because they are low-stakes, quick writes can give students who too often worry about "getting it right" license to take risks. They shift students' mind-sets to embrace creativity and experimentation. Sometimes we have to write junk or be out of step with others to find that creative sweet spot. Quick writes allow for and even encourage this.

Communication

Being able to communicate effectively is a foundational skill we expect from our students. It is how we transfer ideas and information to one another. I know my students have much to say but are often hindered by an inability to express their thoughts as precisely as they wish. The frustration children experience in not being understood has real social, emotional, and behavioral consequence in their lives, in our schools, and in society. When we think about our school day, we may feel limited in our time for students to play with a variety of contexts or styles. Quick writes are one vehicle for offering that creative practice.

I have observed that creativity is an essential component of effective communication—one of what I refer to as "the Seven Cs":

1. Creativity—Piquing the interests of others in fun or unique ways

2. Conciseness—Minimizing the number of words used to convey essential ideas

3. Clarity—Using words that paint a clear picture

4. Compassion—Developing a relationship with your audience and caring about their needs

5. Connection—Knowing your audience and how to convey ideas effectively to them

6. Cognition—Knowing what you are talking about and expertly conveying it to others

7. Cohesion—Expressing ideas that stick together logically and flow smoothly

As you work with some of the quick writes in this book, you may notice how small bursts of writing can lend themselves to addressing these Cs.

Poetry as Wordplay

Poetry is the ultimate form of creative wordplay, yet many kids say they don't like it. Maybe that's because they haven't had enough time to play around with it. They may think poetry is about following specific rules or rhyme patterns when writing or analyzing themes and imagery when reading. What if we give them more time to play with words and ideas so they spend less time worrying about "getting it right?"

MICROPOETRY

Micropoetry was designed to encourage the creation and sharing of poetry on social media platforms like Twitter that restrict text space. Fixed-rule poetry forms such as haiku, tanka, and senryu are common, as is free verse that is limited to available characters. Our quick writes can be a form of micropoetry, limited by time rather than length. Once exposed to a variety of styles, students choose whatever rules, if any, they wish to follow.

WORD POEMS

Working in Janet Frake's fifth-grade class, I share one of my favorite quick write lessons: writing a poem from a single word. I tell students that I often dare myself to write a poem in five minutes inspired by a single word, and that sometimes I try to think of the most boring word I can. Today I share a poem I drafted about chairs. They giggle as I tell them, "If I can write a poem about something this dull, you can too!"

Next I put the word *recess* on the board an invite students to quick write whatever comes to mind. Janet and I observe them feverishly jotting thoughts and connections. The students love to share, and since the composing is so short, there's almost always time. Afterward, they are begging us for more words to try. These kids apparently caught the poetry bug! One writer even incorporates the shape of a slide into his quick write (see Figure 6.2). Now *that* is evidence of play that I love to see!

ACROSTIC POEMS

A more challenging variation on word poems, acrostic poems have the first letter of each line spell out a word or phrase when read vertically. To increase the challenge even further, students might use the last or middle letter of each line. Remember, the idea isn't to

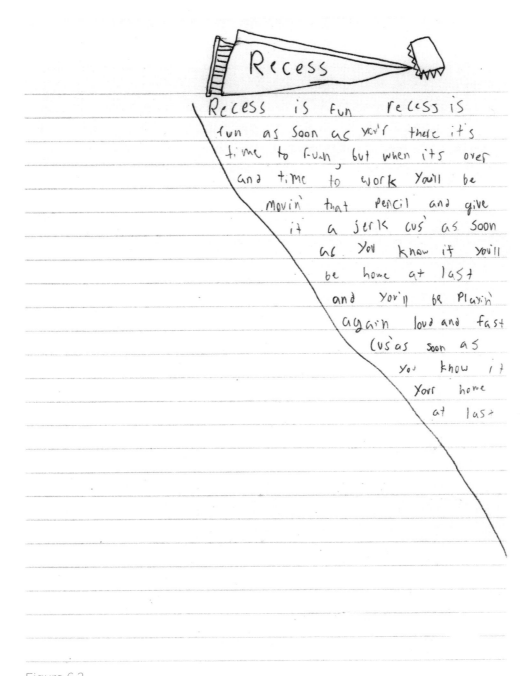

Figure 6.2

Fifth graders create quick write poems from a single word.

create a polished poem but to generate thoughts on paper that link to the word or topic. Many students may not finish in the given time, and that's fine. I love leaving my writers chomping at the bit—it's a good problem to have! Students can always revisit, revise, or re-create their acrostic poem if they choose.

You can generate acrostic words or phrases to align with books, shared experiences, or taught concepts. We share with older students that these quick writes activate their schema on a topic, encouraging them to think about vocabulary and ideas associated with a concept. In one fifth-grade class, we used the format to reflect on a recent unit on fractions. We were amused and enlightened by the varying responses (see Figure 6.3).

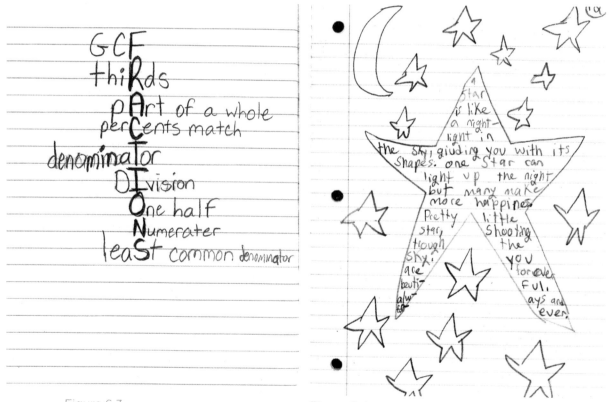

Figure 6.3
Fifth graders activate schema around fractions with a quick write acrostic poem.

Figure 6.4
Fourth graders write impromptu shape poems as quick writes.

SHAPE POEMS

Another quick write that quickly becomes contagious in Kaitie King's fourth grade is shape poetry. Words are vessels for ideas, and this form of poetry can make that abstract concept more concrete for students. I name a shape and invite students to draw a basic outline of it. Then students quick write related words or phrases either inside the shape or on the lines around it. Again, many want to continue experimenting beyond our quick writing time (see Figure 6.4).

We create a cache of shapes for Samantha Esancy's second graders to choose from, and the students quick write poems sparked by their imagination. They want to post their pieces for others to see. We keep our focus on play, not perfection, so students do not revise or edit, but some choose to add more detail to the illustration before sharing (see Figure 6.5).

Figure 6.5
Second graders want to share their quick write shape poems.

DOCUMENTARY POEMS (DOCU-POEMS)

Docu-poems focus on documenting current or historical events. Writers can highlight words and phrases from newspapers, magazines, or copies of primary sources (documents, speeches, archived letters/diaries) and quick write a poem or respond with thoughts and opinions. Classrooms can create a time capsule of poetry to document their school year the way characters in Laura Shovan's book *The Last Fifth Grade of Emerson Elementary* do. In Shovan's book, the students kept a poetry journal to document events each week of the school year. Quick write docu-poems could help our students document a year in their school lives, too.

Guy Meader invites his students to write poems documenting events in their sixth-grade year as part of their quick writes in Google Classroom. We find it interesting to read the events students find significant enough to capture in a poem, as well as each author's approach to poetry (see Figure 6.6).

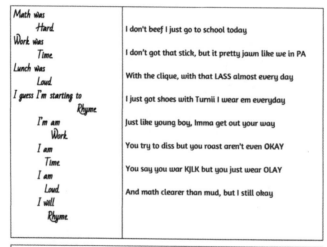

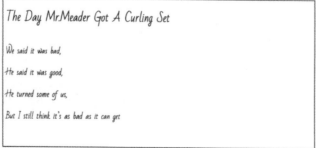

Figure 6.6

Sixth graders write docu-poems about a week in their classroom.

Figurative Language

Figurative language helps to communicate ideas in playful and creative ways that will stay with the reader or listener. It evokes pictures in our minds and awakens our imagination. However, it can be confusing for newcomers to our language or for readers and listeners with less experience. It is helpful if we expose our students to a wide variety of idioms, metaphors, similes, hyperbole, and personification so that they can appreciate and incorporate figurative language into their repertoire of communication and writing skills.

Becky Foster's fifth graders playfully explore meanings and interpretations of figures of speech during several quick write lessons. Doing so helps raise their awareness of figurative language in the books they are reading and in their favorite songs. Becky shares that she is seeing students infuse examples into their other writing assignments, as a result of this playful practice.

The first time I introduce figure of speech quick writes, we all respond to the same phrase and compare ideas. However, we can vary our approach to foster engagement and fun.

- Invite all students to write to the same word or phrase, and see how varied the responses can be for that one example.

- Put examples of the same type of figurative language into a jar, and have students randomly choose a slip and use it to increase the variety and exposure to multiple examples.

- Give students a sheet or Bingo card of multiple examples, and allow them to choose, marking through words after they have been used during the week. This approach gives students choice and allows them to reflect on their decisions.

Take time to explain each form of figurative language and the purpose authors have for using it. Following are some kid-friendly explanations that could become anchor charts and provide a place for student examples to be displayed as mentor texts. I've also collected some samples you could begin with (scan the QR code for access).

https://goo.gl/2eKPAS

Onomatopoeia—a word that mimics or represents the sound of an object or thing. Writers use it to describe sounds in a way that stimulates the reader's senses and helps to pull them into the poem or story (e.g., *buzz, clang*).

Idioms—phrases that have a different meaning from the literal meanings of each word. Writers use them to say things in a colorful way (e.g., *Quake in your boots*). (See Figure 6.7 for an example of an idiom quick write.)

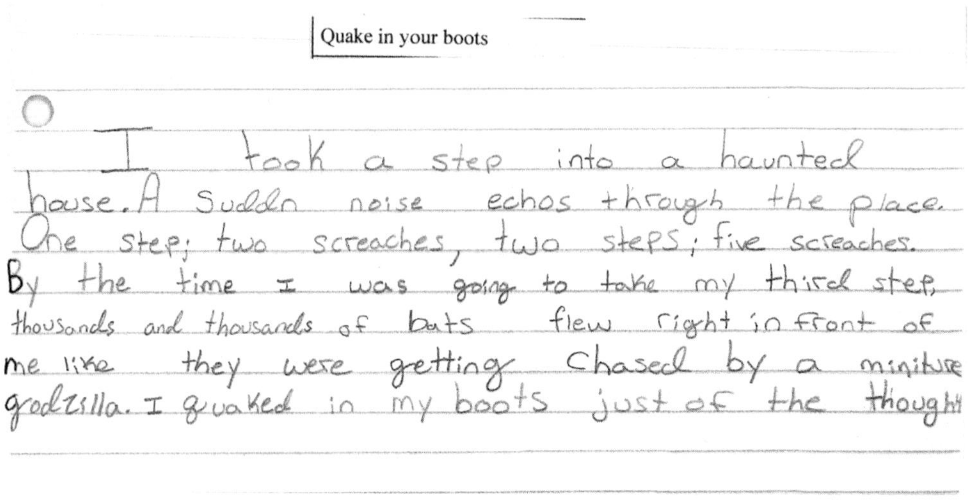

Quake in your boots

I took a step into a haunted house. A sudden noise echos through the place. One step; two screaches, two steps; five screaches. By the time I was going to take my third step, thousands and thousands of bats flew right in front of me like they were getting chased by a miniture godzilla. I quaked in my boots just of the thought

Figure 6.7

Idiom quick write

Metaphors—words or phrases used in a way that is not literal. Writers use them to present ideas in engaging, memorable, and visual ways. (e.g., *My cousin is a couch potato.*) (See Figure 6.8 for an example of a metaphor quick write.)

Similes—phrases that compare two things using *like* or *as*. Writers use them to spark the reader's imagination when thinking about a person, place, or thing by using comparisons the reader is already familiar with (e.g., *He was blind as a bat*).

Hyperbole—using exaggeration to make a point. Writers use it when they feel strongly about something and want the reader to understand the extent of their feelings or opinions (e.g., *I had a ton of homework*).

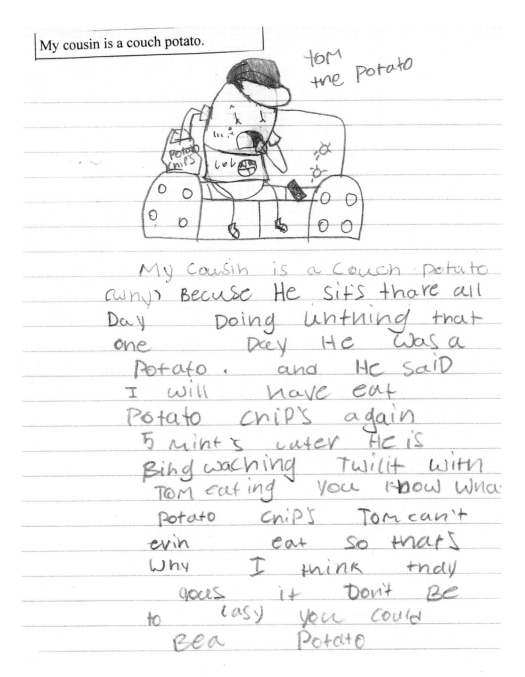

My cousin is a couch potato.

Tom the Potato

My Cousin is a Couch Potato
(why) Becuse He sits thare all
Day Doing unthing that
one Day He was a
Potato. and He said
I will have eat
Potato Chip's again
5 mint's unter He is
Bing waching Twilit with
Tom eating You I'bow Wha
potato chip's Tom can't
evin eat so that's
Why I think tnay
goes it Don't Be
to lasy you could
Be a Potato

Figure 6.8
Metaphor quick write

Figure 6.9

Personification quick write: literal and figurative sketchnote comparison

Personification—giving human qualities or traits to nonliving objects. Writers use it to help readers visualize an object in a specific way that readers can understand and connect with (e.g., *Those books were flying off the shelves*).

Comparing literal and figurative meanings is a creative way to expand our definition of writing while building schema for a concept. (See Figure 6.9 for an example of a visual quick write showing personification.)

Flash Fiction

Flash fiction refers to extremely brief stories that offer some character and plot development. Here are a few ways to incorporate flash fiction into quick writes.

SIX-WORD STORIES

Legend has it that Ernest Hemingway was challenged to write a compelling story in only six words and came up with "For sale: baby shoes, never worn." Whether true or not, the Six-Word Story or Six-Word Memoir has become a popular format for practicing creativity and conciseness in a fun way.

Dan Johnston and Guy Meader's sixth graders take up the challenge for their daily quick writes over the course of a week. They use Google Classroom to post their work, so we compile several examples to share with each other. We can allow students to choose their own genre (memoir, fiction, informational), or we can provide a contextual prompt to spark ideas. If they finish before the time is up, they can continue with additional compositions. Though the pieces are short, we can infer some deeper meanings and complex stories. We also catch glimpses into the real-life issues of some students, especially some of our immigrant families (see Figure 6.10).

Figure 6.10
Sixth graders quick write Six-Word Stories.

SIX WORD STORIES

CAME TO THE US, DIDN'T FEEL UNITED.

At night we were never safe.

Why must you go? Goodbye dad.

HE SHOOTS AND HE SCORES. YAAAAAAAA!

Mom got pregnant. Baby is adorable.

Because is why. All just words.

Read a book, cried at end

TWO-SENTENCE STORIES

Every year around Halloween I see two-sentence horror stories, so we decide to try these with Guy Meader's sixth graders. The idea is to create a spooky scenario that gives enough information for readers to infer what could be happening. Though this quick write spark need not be limited to Halloween, we know it's often what *isn't* said that leaves spooky thinking to the imagination, so the holiday works particularly well. Guy and I quickly observe who can construct complete, complex, and compound sentences and who needs more support and practice. Within five minutes, some students choose to revise or rewrite a story multiple times, contemplating their choices to evaluate their effect. They enjoy sharing their quick short stories and are motivated by their peers to try more (see Figure 6.11).

Two Sentence Stories

I saw a dog in someone's car. It was my dog.

I rubbed a lamp expecting to get three magic wishes from a sparkling jeany. I fell into an endless darkness.

Watching a scary movie with someone is less scary. Unless you live alone.

I was doing laundry and my dog barked. That is when I realized that there was a clown in the basement with me.

I heard the wolf howl, long and sad, I shivered. Then I howled too, announcing to the whole forest that it was mine.

Figure 6.11
Two-Sentence story collection

Some schools take part in the online Five-Sentence Challenge (https://fivesc.net/), where a picture is posted every two weeks and students from all over the world are invited to write five-sentence stories inspired by it. While you may not choose to connect with the online community, you could use the prompts to inspire flash fiction within your classroom or school.

Title Tales

A title gives a hint to the content and genre of a story and can often set the tone. Titles help the reader to predict what the story might be about.

Liz Chadwick and I want to help her fifth graders think more analytically about the titles of books they read, so we try some quick writes focused on envisioning possible stories derived from them. I give them the title *Some Kind of Courage* from Dan Gemeinhart's 2016 middle-grade novel. The students jump in and experiment with genres from personal narrative to realistic fiction to fantasy (see Figure 6.12). After they share we ask them, "How could this quick write activity help you as a reader?" or "How important is a title in helping you predict what you will read?" One student shares that she is going to think more about the titles of books when she's making choices at the library. Another agrees and adds that he didn't really think much about titles before. I've created a collection of book titles to get you started (scan the QR code for access). You can enlist the help of your students to add some of their favorites.

 https://goo.gl/nCFLKi

Opening Lines

We often talk to students about the importance of leads—how those first lines can hook a reader. Becky Foster and I share a quick write with her students that encourages them to pay closer attention to the opening lines of the books they read. We invite them to quick write a story from the opening lines of some middle-grade books. The first time we give students the same line so we can appreciate the diversity that comes from a singular lead. Later, students can select a line randomly from a jar, or more intentionally

10-20²⁰17

One dey I was alone at
home in the night time or day
So I was scared but it really
quite! And I saw or imganed
woifes in the wall right behind
me I turned around and no
One was there I started
to get even more scared and
the lights started to flicker
I was so scared that I
Picked up my Phone and
my Phone died. ~~I wi~~ I opened
the door and checked if anyone
Was out side So I Packed some
clothes and saw my friends
olivia outside I said im Scared
and so was she we both
got are bike, and Stoped
and my friend olivia said,
let me call mom Ok Call
so She called and Picked
up and said are you alright
we both Said\

Figure 6.12
Title Tale quick write on *Some Kind of Courage*

[116]

from a list that we offer them. Scan the QR code for access to a starter collection of opening lines.

   https://goo.gl/WPPGWE

We see the reciprocity of this task as students think about the importance of leads from the stance of a reader as well as a writer. They realize crafting strong leads is not a standalone skill but rather serves as an entry point to the story that follows. From these quick writes, students can see how varied stories can be from a singular hook. Some even play with variations on familiar stories (see Figure 6.13).

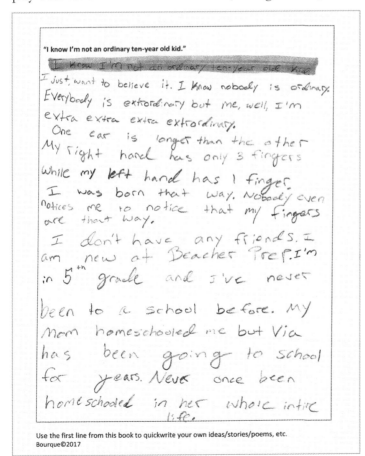

Figure 6.13

Quick Write from opening line of *Wonder*

Dialogue

Guy Meader and I realize the dialogue in his sixth graders' narratives is often confusing for readers; the lack of punctuation and speech tags can make it difficult to follow a conversation. We try dialogue quick writes to give students some creative practice in honing these skills. This activity allows us to see who needs additional supports, lessons, or conferring on dialogue. We do the activity in pairs or trios. Each student writes down a first line of dialogue, then partners exchange papers. They have three minutes to read and respond before exchanging papers once more. Sometimes the conversations are nearly identical, and other times they are wildly different (see Figure 6.14).

We encourage students to reflect on their dialogue-writing skills after this activity by asking them, "What made it easy or difficult to read your partner's dialogue? Did you make it easy for your partner?" Some students find they forgot to include punctuation, while others notice their partners trying a variety of synonyms for *said*. In subsequent quick writes, students can practice dialogue to try balancing action, description, and conversation. Since these activities are not tied to ongoing projects in writing workshop, students play and experiment with a single writing focus rather than multiple craft moves in a larger composition.

Show, Don't Tell

Becky Foster has been working with her fifth graders on this often hard-to-grasp concept. She teaches lessons that encourage her writers to *show* readers what is happening rather than tell them. She coaxes them to share their story through the thoughts, actions, senses, and feelings of their characters and not just description, summary, or opinions.

We decide to create some quick writes to use over several days to isolate and play with this technique. Becky's students select a strip of paper with an emotion written on it. They have five minutes to create a scene that shows rather than tells how their character is feeling. Afterward, they take turns sharing their pieces while their classmates try to infer what emotions they are showing. Student guesses are pretty accurate, and they are beginning to discern similarities and subtle distinctions between feelings and the word choices that define them (see Figure 6.15).

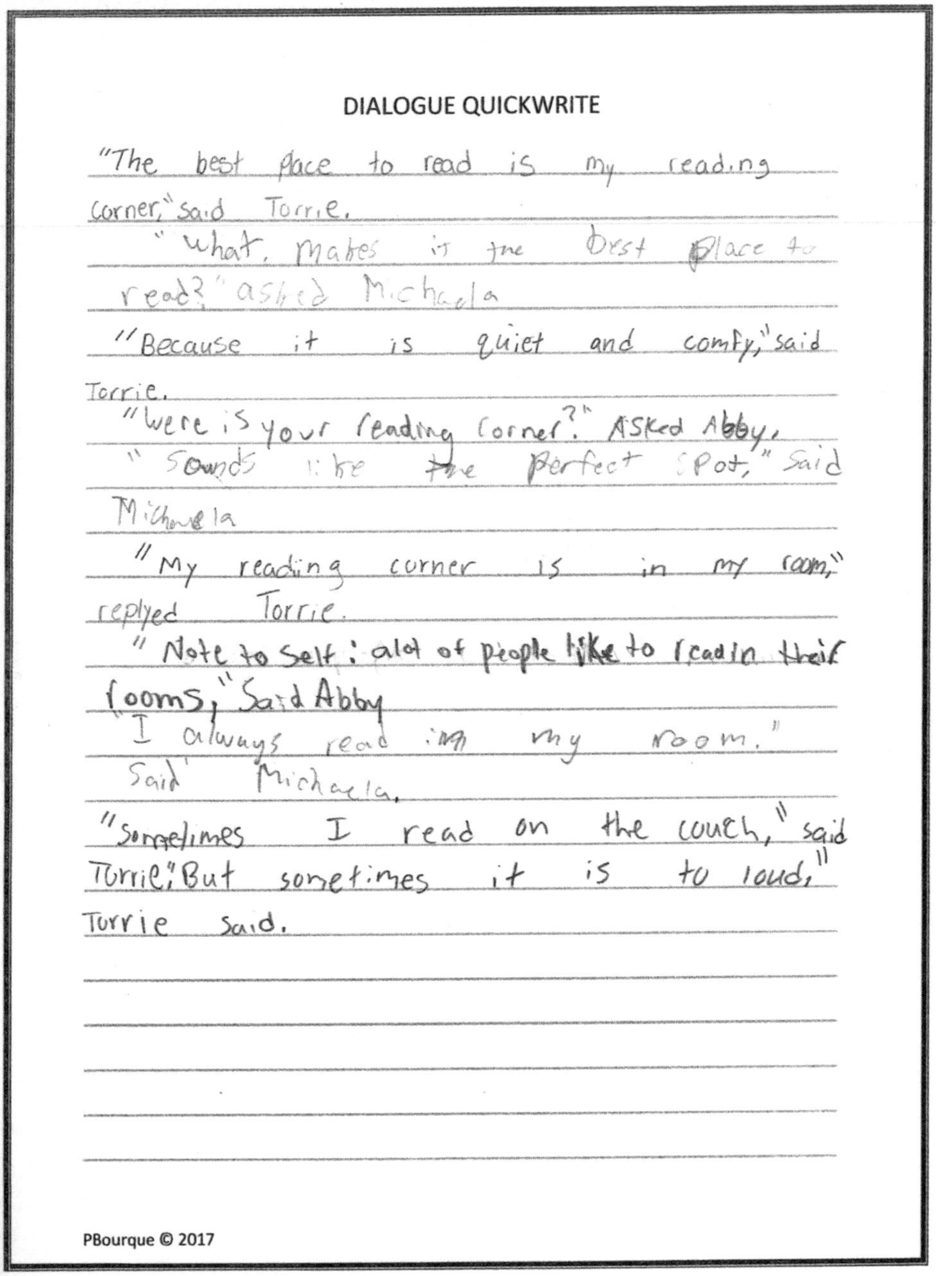

DIALOGUE QUICKWRITE

"The best place to read is my reading corner," said Torrie.

"What makes it the best place to read?" asked Michaela

"Because it is quiet and comfy," said Torrie.

"Were is your reading corner?" Asked Abby.

"Sounds like the perfect spot," said Michaela

"My reading corner is in my room," replyed Torrie.

"Note to self: alot of people like to read in their rooms," Said Abby

"I always read in my room." Said Michaela.

"Sometimes I read on the couch," said Torrie. "But sometimes it is to loud," Torrie said.

PBourque © 2017

Figure 6.14

Students work in partners and trios for dialogue quick writes.

Another quick write involves giving students a setting (such as the woods) that they describe using sensory words. Or we can share a situation (like, for example, grocery shopping) and have students show what is going on around them using their senses while listeners guess the context.

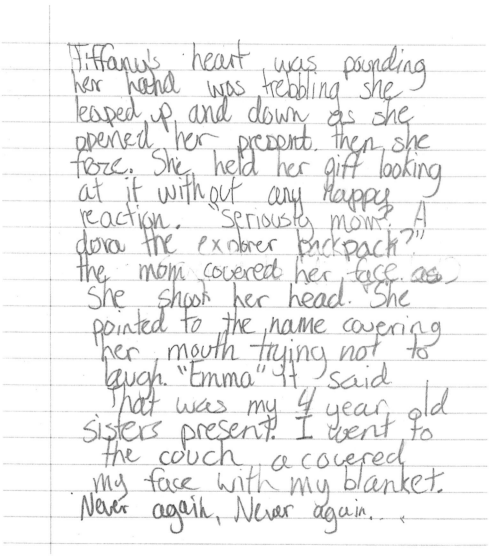

Tiffany's heart was pounding her hand was trebbling she leaped up and down as she opened her present. then she froze. She held her gift looking at it without any happy reaction. "Seriously mom? A dora the explorer backpack?" the mom covered her face as she shook her head. She pointed to the name covering her mouth trying not to laugh. "Emma" it said. That was my 4 year old sisters present. I went to the couch a covered my face with my blanket. Never again, Never again.

Figure 6.15
Students quick write to show, not tell, "Embarrassed and Nervous."

Letter Writing

Many of our students may not have much experience with letter writing. Regrettably, it has fallen prey to the rise of social media, instant messaging, and texting. Research shows there are substantial health benefits to expressive letter writing, including more sleep and less illness (Mosher and Danoff–Burg 2006). Another series of studies shows that writing letters of gratitude increases writers' happiness and life satisfaction while decreasing depressive symptoms (Toepfer 2009, 2012). Quick writing letters to others could be a smart ten-minute investment in the well-being of our students, the spreading of cheer, and the increasing of writing volume.

LETTERS OF GRATITUDE

This type of writing connects us to one another in intimate ways. We contemplate a relationship with someone and reach out to them with words of gratitude. Creating these letters as quick writes takes the emphasis off the formal structure and places it on personal meaning and appreciation. The recipients won't mind that the headings and closings aren't aligned or that the writer forgot to paragraph. They'll genuinely appreciate the warm feelings and gratitude shared on paper. Students may not finish, and they may never deliver the letter, but it is the expression of gratitude through writing that we are valuing.

As Thanksgiving nears, Erin Whitish's fifth graders are asked to pen a letter of gratitude to someone they love. Most choose to write to family members, making the writing task more engaging and personal. We notice it is often the small things for which they are most grateful. These students are eager to share their letters with loved ones (see Figure 6.16).

FRIENDLY LETTERS

Another day, Erin's fifth graders quick write friendly letters. They each contemplate a hero in their lives and then compose a short note to that person. Again, most choose a family member who is dear to them, but the specific details from writers bring tears to our eyes. Imagine the kindness and joy we could spread around this world with more letters like this (see Figure 6.17).

Writing friendly letters to classmates could also become a routine quick write. Some classrooms have a Student of the Week to whom everyone writes a letter. We can recognize staff, volunteers, community members, or visitors.

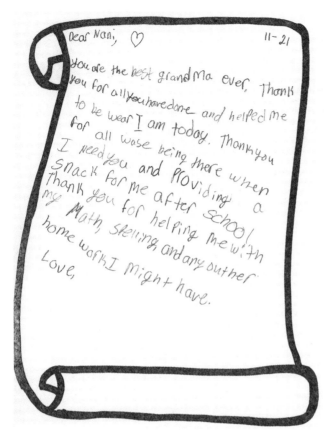

Dear Nani, ♡   11-21

You are the best grandMa ever, Thank you for all you have done and helped me to be wear I am today. Thank you for all wase being there when I need you and providing a snack for me after school. Thank you for helping me with my Math, steuing, and any outher home work I might have.

Love,

Figure 6.16
Quick write: A letter to your hero

Dear dad,

I put you down as my hero because you are an inspiration to me. You want me to be better than you but that's impossible because you are the best person anyone could dream of. I love your work ethic and how much you care for our family. If there's a problem at work or at home you're the guy to fix it. You're known throughout the country of America for all your dedication to our freedom. I know you get tired of all the thank you's you get but, thank you for being yourself.

Love your son

Figure 6.17
Quick write: A letter of thanks to someone you love

For fun and variety, consider the Airmail activity. Invite students to write a question on a paper airplane and send it out in the classroom. Each student scoops up an airmail question and must write a response. Give students two to three minutes to draft a response before the round ends and letters are delivered again. This quick write could easily turn macro if you incorporate several rounds! (A variation of this activity that requires less craftiness is Snowball Fight, where students crumple up their quick write letters like snowballs and toss them.)

Persuasive Letters

A creative way to address childhood challenges and school issues would be to have students write letters to spark change. We can channel complaints, annoyances, and tattles into quick writes that give kids an outlet for their frustration and practice with their writing. Create a "parking lot" poster where students can "park" their grievances, then use these as sparks for quick writing a persuasive letter. Students decide whom to address it to and what they would like to see changed. Remember to emphasize anonymity and respect (e.g., "Dear kids who cut in line" instead of "Dear Jason" or "Dear jerk who cut in line"). We aren't trying to hurt feelings or exact revenge, just persuade others to change or encourage more positive behaviors. Erin's students even practice writing persuasive letters on the same topic to different recipients as a way of exploring how audience can influence composition (see Figure 6.18).

Fan Mail

Most kids want to connect with people they look up to, so fan letters make great quick writes. It can be enlightening for teachers to see who our students admire. I've learned so much about students' interests from reading these letters. The gist is simple: Give students five minutes to quick write a letter to someone of whom they are a fan. We aren't the post office, and we cannot possibly track down addresses and mail these off. Many authors and celebrities no longer even respond to snail mail, tending to rely on social media to connect with fans. If students want them sent I would suggest two ideas: Students take them home, research contact information, and send or post from home; or create a classroom Twitter or Instagram account where students can post snapshots of their letter and tag the recipient. You may need parent permission to post student work, and be aware that not all responses are respectful on social media. Create a hashtag so you can search and

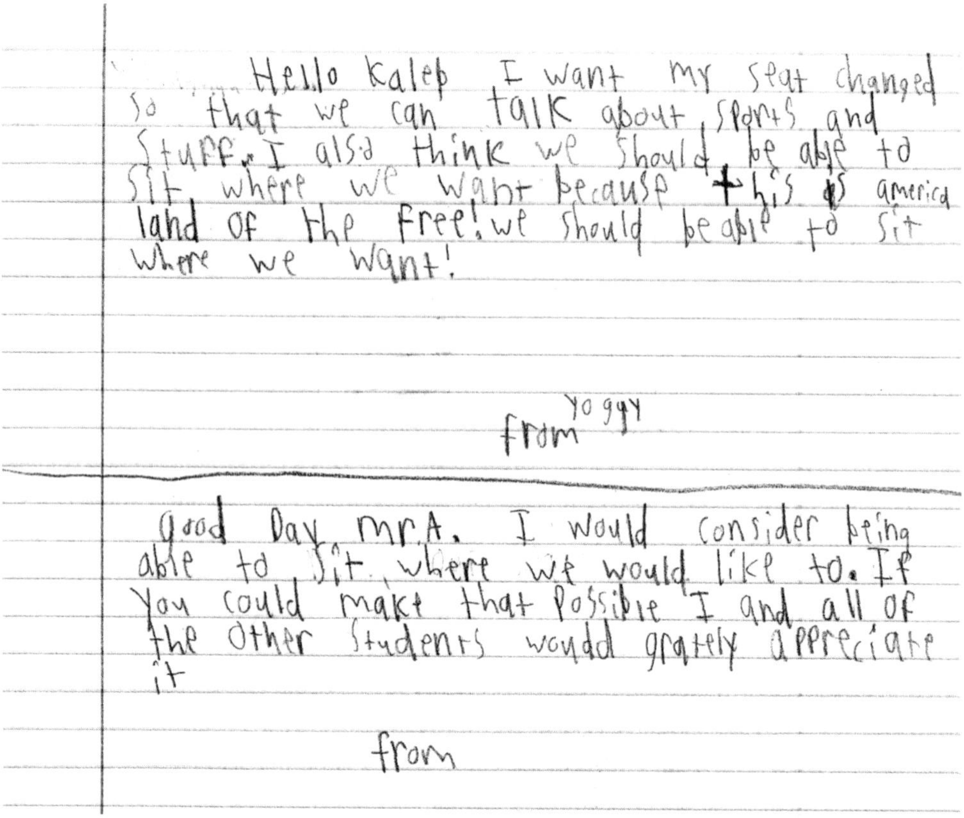

> Hello kaleb I want my seat changed so that we can talk about sports and stuff. I also think we should be able to sit where we want because this is america land of the free! we should be able to sit where we want!
>
> from Yo guy

> Good Day mr.A. I would consider being able to sit where we would like to. If you could make that possible I and all of the other students would grately appreciate it
>
> from

Figure 6.18

Quick write persuasive letter on same topic to two different audiences

track all replies. I have used #AugustaAsks for our district so that all our teachers and students can see posts or responses. I can say from our experience that kid-lit authors are the most likely to write back to their fans (see Figure 6.19).

Quick Wrap

There are so many quick write options and ideas to help our students develop skills for more creative and effective composing and communicating. Jump in and try some, and as you get to know your students, you can select the best sparks to target their needs. Keep in mind that one of their biggest needs may be increasing opportunities to write daily—and enjoy it.

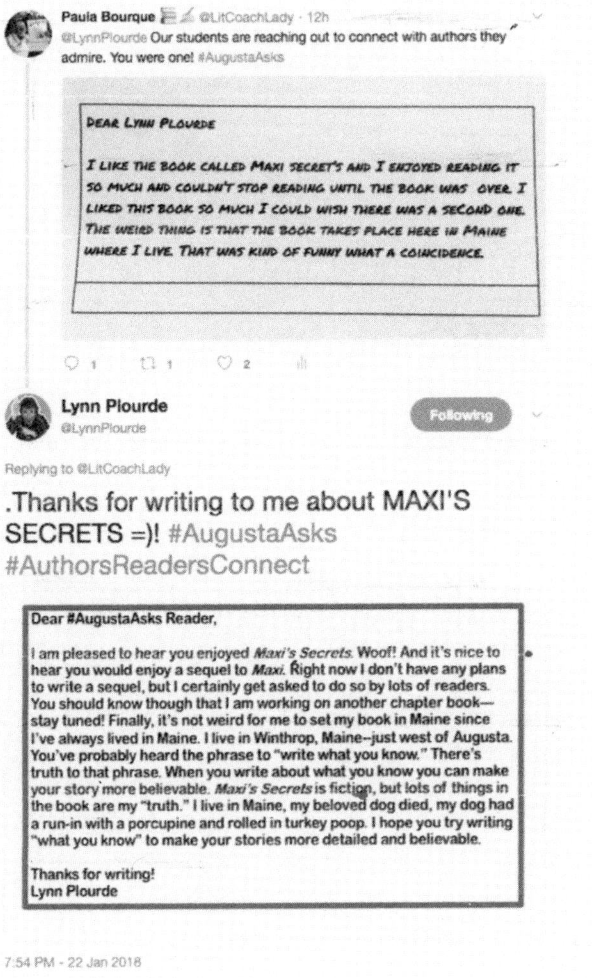

Paula Bourque @LitCoachLady · 12h

@LynnPlourde Our students are reaching out to connect with authors they admire. You were one! #AugustaAsks

DEAR LYNN PLOURDE

I LIKE THE BOOK CALLED MAXI SECRET'S AND I ENJOYED READING IT SO MUCH AND COULDN'T STOP READING UNTIL THE BOOK WAS OVER. I LIKED THIS BOOK SO MUCH I COULD WISH THERE WAS A SECOND ONE. THE WEIRD THING IS THAT THE BOOK TAKES PLACE HERE IN MAINE WHERE I LIVE. THAT WAS KIND OF FUNNY WHAT A COINCIDENCE.

1 1 2

Lynn Plourde @LynnPlourde Following

Replying to @LitCoachLady

.Thanks for writing to me about MAXI'S SECRETS =)! #AugustaAsks #AuthorsReadersConnect

Dear #AugustaAsks Reader,

I am pleased to hear you enjoyed *Maxi's Secrets*. Woof! And it's nice to hear you would enjoy a sequel to *Maxi*. Right now I don't have any plans to write a sequel, but I certainly get asked to do so by lots of readers. You should know though that I am working on another chapter book—stay tuned! Finally, it's not weird for me to set my book in Maine since I've always lived in Maine. I live in Winthrop, Maine–just west of Augusta. You've probably heard the phrase to "write what you know." There's truth to that phrase. When you write about what you know you can make your story more believable. *Maxi's Secrets* is fiction, but lots of things in the book are my "truth." I live in Maine, my beloved dog died, my dog had a run-in with a porcupine and rolled in turkey poop. I hope you try writing "what you know" to make your stories more detailed and believable.

Thanks for writing!
Lynn Plourde

7:54 PM - 22 Jan 2018

Figure 6.19

Quick writes as authentic communication with authors

Quick Write Invite

What does creativity mean to you?

What skills for composing or communicating would you like your students to play with more?

CHAPTER 7

Social-Emotional Quick Writes: Mindfulness, Metacognition, and Mind-Set

 SOCIAL-EMOTIONAL QUICK WRITES

"Educating the mind without educating the heart is no education at all." – Aristotle

Educating the whole child is the goal of elementary teachers I work with. We know academics are important but raising humans is why we are here. Writing can be a vehicle for social emotional learning and awareness.

Focusing on mindfulness, metacognition, and mindset can help integrate hearts and minds. We can plant quick write seeds to stimulate thinking, contemplate identity, encourage empathy, and foster agency.

Figure 7.1

My quick write

QUICK GLANCE: Social-emotional quick writes spark students to build a practice of self-reflection to connect the heart and mind and take control of their learning.

Increasingly, educators are focusing on teaching the whole child and realizing the importance of social-emotional learning. Many believe that academics alone aren't enough to prepare our students for a meaningful life. Teachers looking for ways to incorporate social-emotional learning into busy schedules have found that it doesn't have to be an add-on curriculum. While increasing the volume of writing for students is a crucial goal for quick writes, using it as a vehicle for enhancing their well-being can be an equally important objective. Given the demands of curriculum, we may not have time for extensive units of study with this focus, but we can more easily find five to ten minutes a day to support our students' social-emotional awareness and learning. We use these quick writes to get to know our students on a deeper level to better support their diverse needs and build stronger relationships. Start with some of the ideas and activities I offer here, then think about the experiences of your own students to design quick writes that enhance their social-emotional wellness.

The Three Ms of Social-Emotional Learning

The three areas we have explored for social-emotional awareness and learning are mindfulness, metacognition, and mind-set. There is a great deal of overlap among these three Ms, as they all involve thinking about ourselves, our place in this world, and our identities. Quick writes are an opportunity for that thinking to happen on paper and to reflect and learn as we look back on those traces of thinking.

Mindfulness

Mindfulness helps us to slow down, if even for a few moments, and reconnect with what is happening around and within us. It encourages us to be more aware of how we are feeling and how we frame experiences that shape our reality. I've seen mindfulness described as the pause between stimulus and response—where our choices lie. This pause is often very short for students, with impulsive reactions frequently replacing thoughtful decisions. By its very nature, the act of writing slows down a person's response, if only briefly, as they form an idea and encode it onto paper. We can encourage our students to recognize that this brief time is an opportunity to get in touch with their thoughts and feelings—to contemplate choice. We can train our brains to ask, "What do I notice? What am I feeling? What does this make me think? What does this mean for me?" Students may begin to recognize a default pattern of responding to or interpreting events and develop new insights and awareness into their experiences.

As teachers, we can also practice mindfulness by noticing how our students respond without feeling compelled to act—to be comfortable in what *is* rather than what we wish it to be. This is a Zen practice referred to as "nonattachment to outcomes." Quick writes ask us to observe nonjudgmentally and notice more consciously. See the text box for some of the many potential benefits of mindfulness.

BENEFITS OF MINDFUL PRACTICE

- Increase awareness
- Promote attention and focus
- Strengthen perception
- Develop empathy and compassion
- Reduce emotional stress
- Regulate emotion

MINDFUL MANTRAS

One way to cultivate mindfulness is to plant the seeds of awareness through familiar mantras that remind us to stop and notice. Here are a few that we have used with students recently.

- I am one with nature.

- I am present right now.

- Just breathe.

- I choose an attitude of gratitude, or I am grateful.

- I connect to joy.

"I Am One with Nature" and "I Am Present Now"

Taking students outside to be present in the natural world is a great spark for mindful connection. But don't let weather, time, or geography be a barrier to experiencing the world with your students. There are videos available on YouTube you can use, or you can create your own, as I have done (scan QR codes). I often capture short videos of places I visit that last thirty to sixty seconds. Some are quiet and harmonious; others are loud and hectic. I can take my students to these places with the click of a button and invite them to be present there.

https://goo.gl/CEauy5

One afternoon I share my video of a deer tentatively approaching me in the woods with Kaitie King's fourth graders (scan QR code). I ask the students to put themselves there in the woods, to be present behind the camera. Then I ask them, "What are you seeing? Hearing? Feeling? Wondering?" They write for five minutes about their experience (see Figures 7.2 and 7.3). The idea is to encourage students to notice their experience internally as well as externally, to be fully present in the moment.

https://bit.ly/2yw08yv

Figure 7.2
Videos allow students to "be present" in a variety of locations and situations.

"Just Breathe"

I introduce the idea of breath meditation to students with a video called "Just Breathe" (scan QR code). Afterward I ask them "What are you thinking, feeling, or wondering?" and they respond in writing. Their responses give us an idea of where to go next with mindful practice. Sometimes this meditation brings unexpected streams of thought (see Figure 7.4).

 https://bit.ly/1w6zYyE

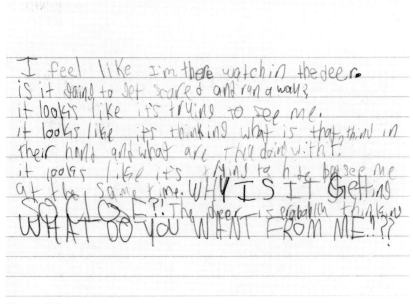

Figure 7.3
Fourth grader quick writes her "in the moment" response to a deer encounter.

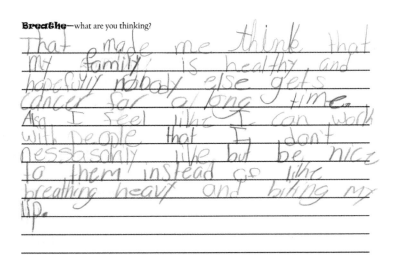

Figure 7.4
Quick write inspired by the "Just breathe" mantra

I am thankful for my dad. He keeps a house over my head and food in my stomach. He's in the military and is currently in Afghanistan. He's fighting for this country, for the safety of all. He's taught me many great things to become the man I am but there is still more time for him to teach me things. He makes me work hard and to be proud of your work no matter what. He doesn't do it for the benefits or to get "thank you's" he does it because he cares about everything and everyone even if he hasn't met you. He does it for his father, his mother, and wife along to impress his five kids all who are nice. He works and he works while he's reaching his days of old to become the best man that he can. I don't know how he does it but he will always care for my family and I.

I'm grateful to our amazing helpers who, evidently, helped restore our power! I'm glad I didn't loose it for long and I would have been grateful for my parents who bought a generator ahead of time 'cause my momma said "I'm glad we got power. If not, Daddy would have started the generator 'cause we got a freezer full of meat we weren't about to lose."

Figures 7.5a and 7.5b
Quick writes using the "I choose an attitude of gratitude" mantra

"I Choose an Attitude of Gratitude" or "I Am Thankful"

We often focus on gratitude in November as our minds and tummies turn toward Thanksgiving, but cultivating a sense of gratitude can enhance our lives year-round. Studies show that keeping a gratitude journal may reap social, psychological, and even physical benefits (Emmons 2010). Incorporating frequent quick writes of gratitude can help our students to celebrate what is meaningful to them. They tend to start big and obvious with their objects of thanks, but with practice they begin to notice the little things in life that bring them meaning (see Figures 7.5a and 7.5b).

"I Connect to Joy"

Gratitude and joy are similar but not exactly the same. We are grateful for people, places, and things, and we find joy during experiences with them. Encouraging students to recount moments of joy in their life and memorializing them in a quick write can spark feelings of gratitude and well-being. Writing about joy triggers some of the same feelings of happiness and love that we experienced the first time. Although many of our students deal with heartache and trauma, they almost always find moments of joy that quick writes can preserve (see Figures 7.6a and 7.6b).

What brings Me Joy is when my dad comes home from work. Whenever he comes home and opens the door. my sister, My baby brother and I, rush towards My dad and give him a big hug, even my dog Jumps on him, and my brother Stands and wants My dad to pick him up.

JOY

A time when I felt joy was when I could learn how to ride a bike. It wasn't a major event but it was a time that I was proud of doing. I could feel joy inside of me. I was excited that I could learn how to ride one. It made me feel joy because some people take weeks to learn to ride one but it took me a few minutes. I think of myself as a quick learner, well on some stuff. Anyways it was a best moment in my life that I could learn to ride a bike. That is why I felt joy that day, and I will always remember that moment.

Figures 7.6a and 7.6b
Quick writes using the "I connect to joy" mantra

ROLE PLAYING

When we are mindful of the thoughts and feelings of others, we develop empathy and compassion. These are two social-emotional skills that we would do well to nurture in this next generation of citizens. There are many resources designed to kindle these traits, but role-playing quick writes offer students practice walking in the shoes of others or grappling with moral issues to problem solve the question "What would I do?" Try some of these role-playing scenarios as quick write lessons (see Figure 7.7 for student examples):

- An older student keeps picking on one of your friends on the playground.

- One of your friends tells you to stop being friends with another student.

- You loan someone your pencil, and they lose it.

- A new student who seems about to cry comes into your class.

- The teacher asks you to pick up the mess by your desk, but someone else made it.

- You hear some students laughing about the snacks that another student brings to school.

- You are assigned a learning partner you don't like very much.

- One of your friends won't talk to you and is ignoring you.

- Every time you try to talk to your friends during lunch someone interrupts you.

- You see a friend taking money out of someone else's backpack.

- The whole class has to stay in for recess because they got so noisy.

- You notice the student sitting next to you sneaking some of your snack.

- You forgot to do your homework, and your teacher asks you where it is.

- Someone cuts in front of you when you line up in class.

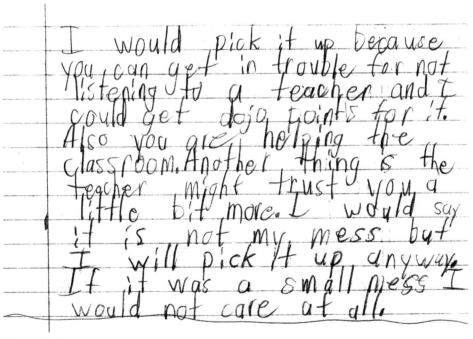

Figure 7.7
Role-playing with quick writes

There are dozens of resources and exercises that can encourage your students to be more mindful. I have pulled some together in a Padlet to help (scan the QR code). I invite you to explore and use these in your classrooms. The quick writes students then do in response offer yet another opportunity for students to be present and mindful as the words flow onto their papers.

 https://bit.ly/2A4zOIW

Metacognition

Metacognition is the awareness and understanding of our thought process. "Thinking about thinking" is a crucial skill students must grasp in order to take charge of their learning. Metacognition is often what makes the difference between engagement and compliance. Students who are metacognitive are often more resilient learners. They can monitor their own thinking to manage frustrations, face down challenges, and contemplate alternative approaches. Metacognition doesn't come naturally to many students, so quick writes are a good way to practice the skill.

BENEFITS OF METACOGNITIVE PRACTICE
• Understand how we learn best
• Enhance self-awareness
• Increase engagement
• Regulate behavior
• Boost resilience

EXIT SLIPS

One of the most common forms of classroom quick writes is the exit slip. These are opportunities for students to share their thinking, assess their learning, or ask lingering questions. We can give students a sample problem or question from the lesson and ask them to share their thinking or process (see Figure 7.8). These quick writes may be specific to a lesson or more generic exercises to spark self-reflection. Teachers can use them as formative assessments, and students can use these to strengthen metacognitive skills.

Mark has _____ watermelons. He cuts each watermelon in half.

How many pieces does he have now?

Explain how you would solve this problem.

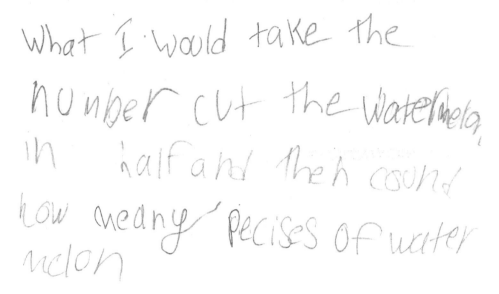

What I would take the number cut the watermelo, in half and then cound how meany pecises of water melon

Figure 7.8

Exit slips spark a habit of self-reflection for thinking and learning.

Here are some generic quick write prompts to consider:

- What did you learn today?

- What is still tricky, confusing, unclear?

- What are you wondering?

- What were you feeling during the lesson?

- What will you try to remember?

SELF-REFLECTIONS

Similar to exit slips, self-reflections invite students to contemplate their learning, strategies, and approaches after completing a unit of study, an assignment, or even a day of learning. Teachers can frame these prompts to help students appreciate their efforts more mindfully. We don't want students to wait passively for others to evaluate their work; we want them to develop a sense of agency in self-evaluation and reflection. This reflective writing raises awareness and helps make learning stick, increasing the likelihood of transferring those skills and behaviors to other situations (see Figure 7.9).

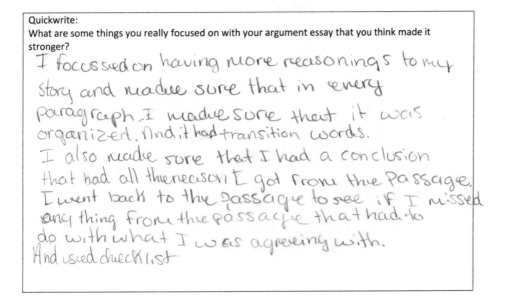

Figure 7.9

Students reflect on intentional decisions and strategies that enhance their learning.

Here are some sparks for self-reflection quick writes:

- What did you focus on to make this work stronger?

- What do you want me to notice about this work you are submitting?

- What is something new you tried with this work?

- What makes this your best effort?

- What did you learn today/this week that you want to remember?

- If your family asks "What did you learn today?" what will you say?

There are also opportunities to self-reflect with quick writes separate from specific lessons or assignments. Part of being metacognitive is to be aware of how you approach not only learning but life itself. Awareness of our feelings and attitudes can help us to understand the choices we make and behaviors we choose. Inviting students to contemplate aspects of self-awareness, self-management, and social awareness can support their social-emotional growth. Try some of these prompts as sparks for self-awareness unrelated to specific lessons or assignments:

- How do I describe myself to others?

- What emotions do I feel most often?

- What are my strengths?

Being a leader? A leader is someone others can look up to and believe in for some it is a parent or friend.
For others people online or in a fictional story

But how to be a leader is the real question. Well for everyone it is different maybe being a leader for some is standing tall and having a hard shell or being soft kind and hidden

For me it is in between being a leader means helping even if it isn't appreciated or being someone to talk to when need.

Being a leader is more than a title it is something you work for. Giving those two seconds of your time to someone else

Figure 7.10
Quick writes for self-awareness and self-direction

- What are my challenges?

- What am I good at? How do I know?

- How can I be a leader whom others respect? (See Figure 7.10.)

These prompts are effective sparks for self-management quick writes:

- What goals do I have for myself this month/semester/year?

- What challenges will I have to overcome or work on?

- What can my teacher do to support me?

- What can my class do to support me?

- What can I do if I am feeling frustrated?

- What interest or passions do I want to explore on my own? (See Figure 7.11.)

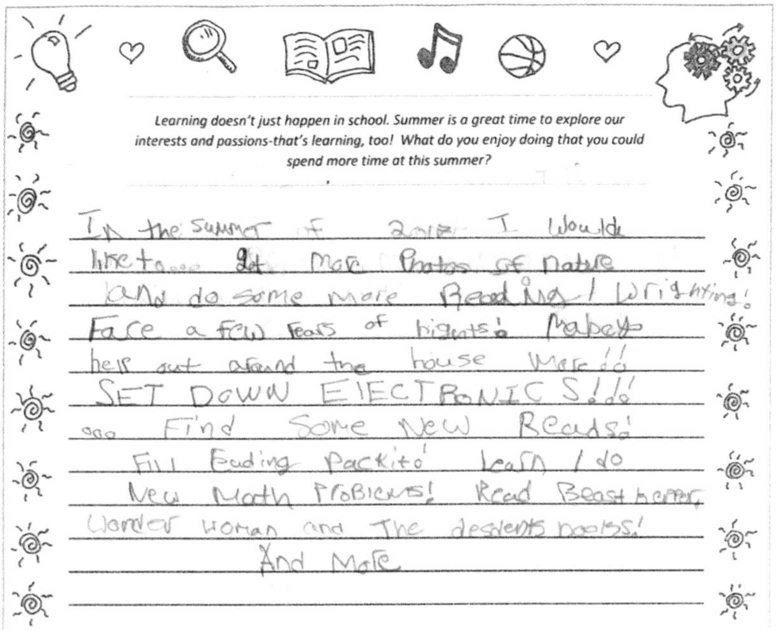

Figure 7.11
Quick writes for self-management

Use these prompts to spark social awareness and intradependence during quick writes:

- How can I best contribute to this class?

- How can I support others with their goals?

- How do I show respect to others?

- How do I tune in to the needs of others?

- What could I say to a friend who is frustrated?

- How can I be a good partner to someone? (See Figure 7.12.)

- How can I be open to learning from others?

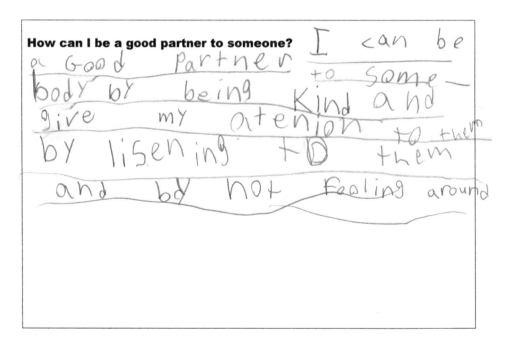

How can I be a good partner to someone? I can be a Good Partner to some-body by being Kind and give my atenion to them by lisening to them and by not fooling around

Figure 7.12

Quick writes for fostering intradependence

Mind-Set

Mind-set refers to the beliefs and attitudes we hold about ourselves. Carol Dweck's research (Dweck 2008) helped us to understand those with a fixed mind-set believe that their qualities are predetermined (i.e., "fixed") traits over which they have no control. By contrast, those with a growth mind-set believe they can improve their skills through effort and see failure and challenge as part of the growth process. Most people do not fall solidly into one camp or the other.

Those with a fixed mind-set avoid challenges, give up more easily, and see effort as useless. Those with a growth mind-set embrace challenges, persist when things get tough, and believe their effort will pay off. Quick writes that encourage students to reflect on their beliefs and attitudes about themselves can make them aware of their mind-set, and awareness is the first step toward action.

REFLECTING ON IDENTITY

Our identity is the combination of how we see ourselves and how others see us and is closely related to self-image and self-esteem. We want our students to develop healthy personal identities so that they feel empowered with a positive mind-set. As teachers, it is advantageous to understand how students see and define themselves, not only as learners but as people, to understand their motivation and mind-set. Try some of these quick write sentence stems to spark thinking:

- I'm the kind of reader who . . . (see Figure 7.13)

- I'm the kind of writer who . . .

- I'm the kind of student who . . .

- I'm the kind of classmate who . . .

- I'm the kind of friend who . . .

EXPLORING BELIEFS ABOUT OURSELVES

Beliefs express our way of thinking and looking at things or ourselves that may, or may not, be based on factual evidence. Our beliefs influence our behavior, even if we aren't aware of it. Becoming more aware can help us to recognize how our beliefs shape our decisions, motivations, and behavior. If you believe you are capable and competent, you

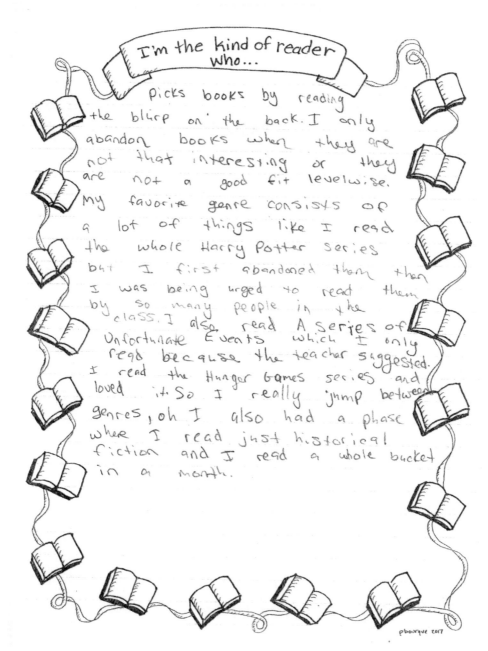

I'm the kind of reader who...

picks books by reading the blurb on the back. I only abandon books when they are not that interesting or they are not a good fit levelwise. My favorite genre consists of a lot of things like I read the whole Harry Potter series but I first abandoned them then I was being urged to read them by so many people in the class. I also read A Series of Unfortunate Events which I only read because the teacher suggested. I read the Hunger Games series and loved it. So I really jump between genres, oh I also had a phase where I read just historical fiction and I read a whole bucket in a month.

pbourque 2017

Figure 7.13

Quick writes for understanding self-identity

may embrace challenges. If you believe mistakes are part of learning, you may be more willing to take risks. However, if you believe you aren't smart enough or a task is too hard, you may not see a point in putting in much effort. Beliefs shape our mind-set, and if we aren't aware of them, they can easily sabotage our learning.

Quick writes can help students reflect on their personal beliefs. They can be shared to promote empathy and understanding or kept private to protect the authors. We can't convince students to change their beliefs, but we can invite them to reflect on how they may be helpful or hurtful in their lives. There are endless questions we can pose to our students to encourage this self-awareness. Here are a few:

- What are five words that best describe you?

- Should students be challenged?

- Can mistakes make us smarter? (See Figure 7.14.)

- What does it mean to be a good student?

- Does effort (hard work) make a difference for everyone?

- What motivates you?

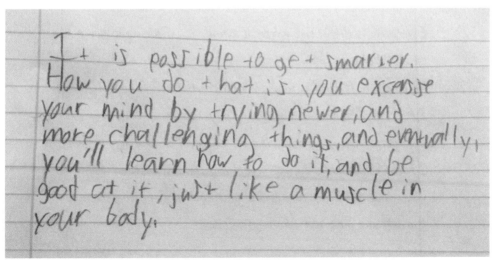

Figure 7.14
Quick writes can spark reflection on our personal beliefs.

FOSTERING GROWTH MIND-SET

There are countless resources for introducing students to the theory of growth mind-set; a simple Internet search will set you right up. Lessons that explicitly teach this concept can have strong implications for our students' learning, and we can keep that awareness going throughout the year if we revisit it frequently using quick writes. Here are some sparks to help students develop a growth mind-set:

- I used to _____, but now I _____.

- I can see that I'm better at _____ than I used to be.

- Some things that used to be hard for me were _____.

- When I have assignments that are hard in the future, I'm going to remember _____.

- I think of mistakes as _____.

- How do I feel when I try something that is difficult? (See Figure 7.15.)

How Do I Feel When I Try Something That is Difficult?

Everyone is different when it comes to challenges some like to avoid the problem.
Go around it, find a new way to solve it, or face it head on.
I feel like I face mine in a multiply was. And the way I councer them is by knowing at the end of the day I tried.
I feel like a challenge is something that is needed in life to make you stronger and show you how to face something.
But others may not like a challenge.

Figure 7.15
Quick writes to foster a growth mind-set

- What do I do when something is too easy?

- What is something that really challenged me today?

- What is something I have learned from a mistake?

- What can I do differently tomorrow to help me?

REFRAMING

Mind-sets are created by our experiences and therefore influence how we frame those experiences. We don't experience an objective reality; we create a narrative that reflects our interpretation of it. We can get locked into a narrative that limits our potential for growth. What if we could reframe some of the stories we tell ourselves to break out of a default mode of thinking and embrace other possibilities?

"Reframing is about changing the meaning we give to events, not necessarily changing the events themselves" (Greene and Grant 2003). Quick writes are a great way to explore and practice reframing because we don't have to invest a lot of time or energy into extended writing from a fixed frame. We aren't drafting positions to persuade others; our only purpose is to play with or adjust our own perspectives, perceptions, or assumptions. We can try on different frames. We can see where our thinking takes us.

Reframing isn't just an interesting writing exercise; it is empowering. When students begin to understand that experiences don't define who they are or how they must respond, they are more likely to develop a growth mind-set and a sense of agency in school and life.

One way to reframe thinking is through a "half-full or half-empty" exercise. In a fifth-grade classroom, I discussed a recent storm that led to extensive power outages. I asked the students if there's any way the storm could have been a good thing, and no one could think of an example. I asked them if they'd heard the expression "Is the glass half-full or half-empty?" To my great surprise, no one had. I took a student's water bottle and asked, "Who would say this bottle is half-full?" Many students raised their hands. I followed, "Who would say this bottle is half-empty?" Many other students raised their hands. "Who is right?" I asked. "We both are," some suggested, while others looked on quizzically. We discussed how the answer to the question reflects how you frame circumstances. We often think of people who choose to see the glass half-full as positive and optimistic and those who see it half-empty as negative and pessimistic.

Returning to the discussion about the storm, one student finally thought of a silver lining: "Well, I did get to go out to eat with my mémère." After that, several students were able to acknowledge some enjoyable moments that resulted from the storm. We immediately saw the power of reframing a circumstance for which they had no control into a somewhat positive experience.

In addition to reframing specific events or experiences, we can give our students opportunities to practice reframing with more generic statements they can apply to their own lives and experiences. We share quotes from philosophers or authors who may inspire them to reframe thoughts more positively. Here are a few sparks to get started (scan the QR code for more):

- Hard is not the same as impossible.

- It could be worse.

- You have everything you really need.

- Comparison leads to unhappiness.

- What doesn't challenge you, doesn't change you. (See Figure 7.16a.)

- "For every minute you are angry you lose sixty seconds of happiness." (Ralph Waldo Emerson)

- "Folks are usually about as happy as they make their minds up to be." (Abraham Lincoln)

- "The best way to cheer yourself is to try to cheer someone else up." (Mark Twain; see Figure 7.16b)

- "You miss 100 percent of the shots you don't take." (Wayne Gretzky)

- "If you dream it, you can do it." (Walt Disney)

 https://goo.gl/nThZjo

Thinking and responding beyond our usual default settings is challenging. Don't expect students to find many of these quick writes easy. I compare the process to lifting weights: If it is always effortless, there is little growth. It is in the purposeful practice that students can train their brains to build strength and flexibility with thinking.

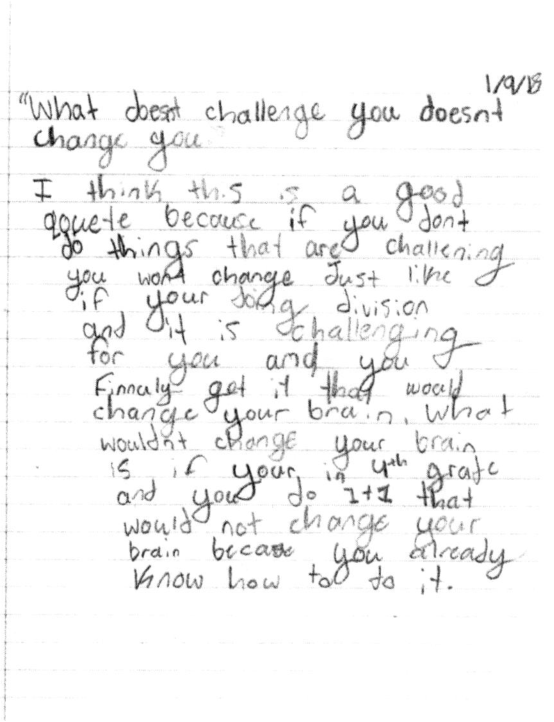

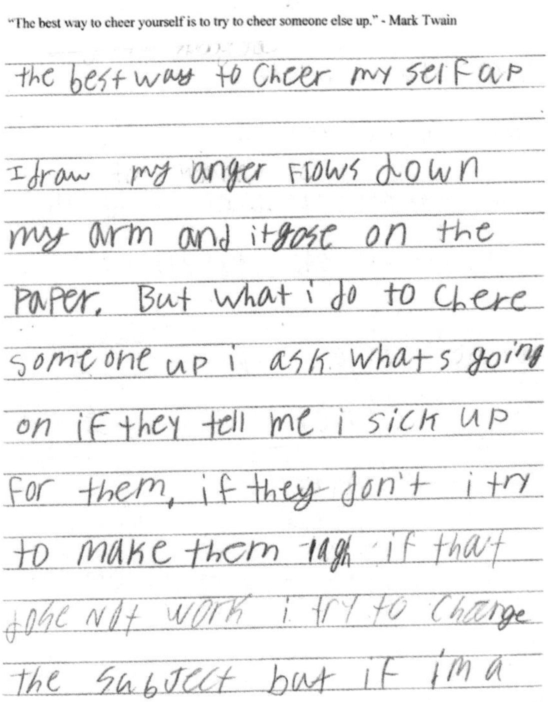

"The best way to cheer yourself is to try to cheer someone else up." - Mark Twain

1/9/18

"What doesn't challenge you doesn't change you"

I think this is a good qquote because if you don't do things that are challening you won't change just like if your doing division and it is challenging for you and you Finnaly get it that would change your brain, what wouldn't change your brain is if your in 4th grade and you do 1+1 that would not change your brain becase you already know how to do it.

the best way to cheer my self ap

I draw my anger Flows down my arm and it goes on the paper. But what i do to chere someone up i ask whats going on if they tell me i sick up for them, if they don't i try to make them lagh if that done not work i try to change the subject but if im a

Figure 7.16a and 7.16b
Responding to quotes to practice reframing

Quick Wrap

While the social-emotional quick writes in this chapter may focus on what many consider noncognitive skills, I would argue that these skills are just as important as cognitive ones for education. We can boost the volume and practice of writing while increasing self-awareness when we combine writing and reflection. Start with some of the ideas and activities I offer here, then think about the experiences of your own students to design quick writes that can enhance their mindfulness, metacognition, and mind-set.

Quick Write Invite

How does your school address social-emotional learning for students?

What is an issue you could reframe to gain another perspective?

CHAPTER 8

Teacher Quick Writes: Inspiring Learning and Leading

TEACHING QUICK WRITES

The BEST writing teachers are _writing_ teachers! When we walk the talk we know the path. So what's the biggest obstacle? TIME? CONFIDENCE? PURPOSE? Let's put scaffolds in place (the way we do for our students) to help us overcome these obstacles. The time can be short. You don't have to do it alone – we can create a community. We can create meaning and purpose with an authentic audience or private exploration. We need to make it easy to build a habit. We just need a SPARK to light a FiRE!

Figure 8.1

My quick write

QUICK GLANCE: Teacher quick writes spark reflection, empathy, and understanding while cultivating a collaborative community and building a writing habit.

I don't believe we can take any professional development course on writing that matches the growth and understanding we get from developing a writing habit. Writing stretches our thinking, expands our repertoire for teaching, brings awareness to the craft, and instills empathy for our students; it is indeed a skill we learn best by doing. However, I also realize that building a habit takes time, which many teachers find hard to carve out consistently. Providing scaffolds and supports are often just as helpful to teachers as they are to students. I offer several invitations in this chapter as sparks to encourage your own quick write habit!

Quick Write Invite

Take three minutes and quick write a response to the following question: How can being a writer impact the way I teach writing?

I've looked for ways to make consistent writing more accessible for teachers in our district, and quick writes fit the bill perfectly. They have no burdensome time commitment and invite us into a community of writers. The activities I suggest here make participation easier and more enjoyable for all staff. I offer sparks to stimulate thinking and writing and offer opportunities to share our words with supportive colleagues as an authentic audience. I've tried two approaches this year (collaborations and challenges) that have encouraged several teachers to jump into writing with a small investment of time and lots of support.

Collaborative Quick Writing

Because our staff is spread out over several schools in our district, we looked for ways to collaborate online. This approach fosters intradependence among teachers who may otherwise feel isolated. Thank goodness for Google! We can work together on a Google Doc to create a piece of writing that doesn't require a large commitment from any one contributor but exemplifies that concept of *stronger together* for our teaching community (see Figure 8.2). We are teachers of writing who write with and for one another. Using a shared document makes it easy to begin a collaborative quick write. I send the Google Doc out to staff with the understanding that their contributions are voluntary and anonymous. They always have the option of keeping their writing private or sharing with others, which

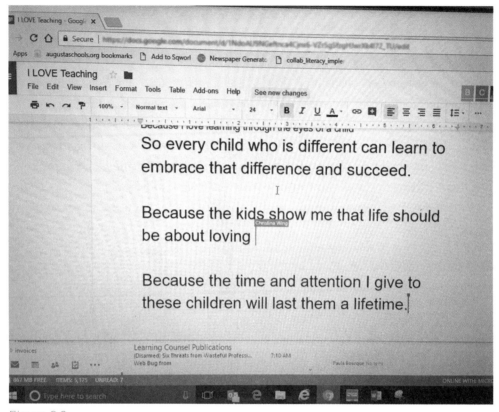

Figure 8.2
Teachers collaborate online to compose group quick writes.

I make clear before they begin. Teachers have a day or two to add their responses, then I print copies of the poem-like pieces to post around the schools.

In selecting the *sparks* for these collaborative pieces, I try to think about purpose and audience. Sometimes the pieces are posted where students, parents, and community members can engage with them (see Figure 8.3); other times they are intended for our staff members to enjoy or contemplate. Sometimes they are designed to inform or explain; other times to promote collegiality or encourage empathy. I particularly enjoy posting our published pieces where we have a captive audience to peruse them (see Figure 8.4)!

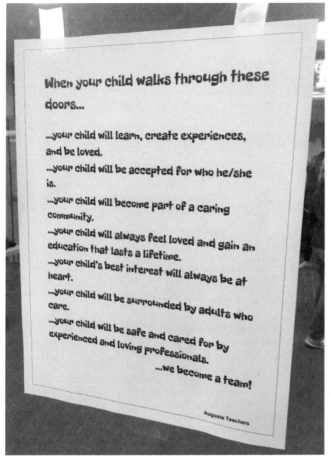

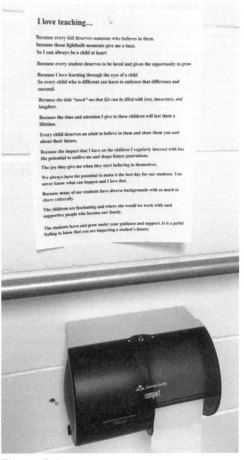

Figure 8.3
Sharing collaboration quick writes with school community

Figure 8.4
Sharing collaboration quick writes with a captive audience

I also formed a Facebook group for our district, Augusta Teachers Write, where we post collaborative quick writes. Teachers' individual writing contributions are small, but the reflection and collaborative composition are impactful. We not only share our thinking but get to know one another more personally, which strengthens the bonds of our community (see Figure 8.5). These types of quick writes can be just the spark teachers need to ignite their writing and feel welcomed into a writing community. The key is to start wherever they are and build on what they are comfortable with to kindle a healthy habit.

Quick Write Invite
What ideas do you have for launching collaborative quick writes with your colleagues?

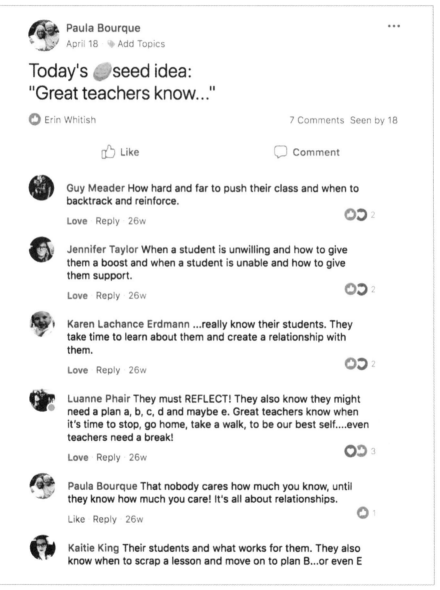

Figure 8.5

Quick write collaborations from our group Facebook page

COLLABORATION SPARKS

There are other collaborative writing sparks we can use to touch off a supportive writing community. We think about our purpose, potential audience, and personnel to help us get started. We can use a shared document, a Facebook post, or an Instagram or Twitter hashtag as a collaborative platform. Be creative. Have fun. Get writing! Here are a few sparks to get you started.

To promote inspiration:

- I teach because . . .

- I write because . . .

- Great teachers know . . .

- When I look into the faces of my students . . . (see Figure 8.6)

When I look into the faces of my students...

I see worry. I see fear for where their next meal might come from. I see innocence. I see the future. But most of all I see hope.

I see wonder. I see resilience. I see kindness. I see a desire to be heard and seen and learn. I also see hope.

I see hope. The hope for our future walking around in this precious person. The hopes of a parent who want the best for their bundle of joy. The hope of a child for acceptance and love. My hopes that I can meet their needs and make a difference in their lives.

I see the people who will be running the world. Best to give them the most powerful tools possible to do some good with that responsibility.

I see so much hope. These innocent children (ELLs)have experienced more than we could ever imagine. They are eager to learn, and dream of better lives for their families.

I see potential.

I see eyes searching for more. More learning, more fun, more love, more food....more, more, more. I want to give them more.

I see pain. Just below the surface are tears that are held back. They know if they let the one tear go, there will be many more, and they may not be able to stop. The pain is about anxiety, fear, uncertainty, upheaval, abuse, neglect, hunger, cold, and longing

#AugustaTeachersWrite

Figure 8.6
Collaboration quick write to spark inspiration

- If the public only knew . . .

- The best teachers . . .

- When I feel down or defeated, I . . .

- I am inspired by . . .

- I love teaching because . . .

- A trait that all great teachers have is . . .

For celebration:

- The best part of teaching is . . .

- I know I've succeeded when . . . (see Figure 8.7)

I know I've succeeded when...

I see the light come on in my students' eyes, I hear them talking about the concept, they use the concept in another way, they work hard, they're nice to each other, and I've tried my best!

when I feel a sense of pride after completing a daunting task. The sense of also feeling positive, happy and grateful even during difficult journeys.

my students are still talking about the topic and are anxious for the next lesson. I also feel successful when I'm exhausted at the end of the day????

Pride is a huge factor. Seeing students proud of their final product and feeling proud of lessons I design. Another factor is reputation. When students from younger grades introduce themselves and ask to be in my class or parents want their younger children to be in my class eventually. Lastly, there is success in lasting relationships.

when that "a-ha" look washes over faces. When they are eager to share their work with others. When there are more "teachers" in the room than me. When they feel satisfied, but hunger for more.

when my kids are happy and having a good time and at the end of the day they leave with smiles and hugs and *I love yous*! Also, when other teachers inquire about something I do or have done and when I can easily talk to and share ideas/opinions with other teachers!

when a student explains why they are having trouble and asks for a support that will make them more successful!

Figure 8.7
Collaboration quick write to spark celebration

- There is nothing better than . . .
- Our school ROCKS because . . .
- When you visit our school, I hope you notice . . .
- A teacher I admire is . . .
- At the end of a school (day/week/year) I feel . . .
- In my class this month I celebrated . . .
- Success looks like (sounds like) . . .
- You know you are a nerdy teacher if . . .

For contemplation:

- Holidays are all about . . .
- Summers are a time for . . .
- When I read . . .
- When I write . . .
- I am most happy when . . .
- We all need time to . . . (see Figure 8.8)
- You haven't really lived until . . .
- Number three on my bucket list is . . .
- The thing that surprised me most about teaching is . . .
- Teaching has taught me . . .

Quick Write Invite

Take three minutes to quick write a response to one of the preceding stems. What did you notice about your thinking?

"We all need time to..."

...be outside and connect with nature. It is humbling, and even comforting, to be part of something so immense...and appreciating that we are but a tiny piece of this world that doesn't revolve around us. Everything is connected.

...relax, have fun, and reconnect with ourselves through whatever makes us feel rejuvenated and content–

...laugh. Allow a hearty belly laugh because we have little control and what other option is there?

... to feel the pull of gravity keeping us grounded. To be quietly held captive under fuzzy dogs. Living life right now without wishing or wanting.

...experience life for how beautiful it is.

...sit in silence and be more mindful. Enjoy time with loved ones. Most importantly be thankful for the things we do have!

...be with loved ones....away from technology (as I type) to reconnect and really listen.

...take care of our health. Exercise, good nutrition, rest, and WATER. If we don't take care of ourselves, we cannot take care of others. Put the oxygen mask over yourself first, and then assist the people around you.

#AugustaTeachersWrite

Figure 8.8

Collaboration quick write to spark contemplation

Teacher Quick Write Challenge

Composing our own short pieces of writing involves a slightly greater time commitment than collaborative writing. We also use an online platform to share and respond to writing in our district. I created a Google Classroom called "Teacher Quick Writes" for our interested staff members. Each day for a month, I post an assignment/challenge in the Google Classroom as a spark to kindle teacher responses. Sometimes the sparks are short passages or poems to read, videos to watch, or quotes to contemplate. I ask teachers to write for three minutes. If they choose to write for more than three minutes, that's fine, but they need to differentiate "overtime writing" with a different font style or color so that others won't be intimidated by the length of their work.

Keeping the writing short and sweet is key to getting and retaining writers for this challenge. Nearly everyone I've approached has responded "Oh, I can write for three minutes!" and stuck with it. I start the challenge with a series of themed days.

- Mindful Mondays (inspire or motivate as we kick off our week)

- Topical Tuesdays (respond to topics related to education)

- Wondering Wednesdays (kindle curiosity about ideas in or out of the classroom)

- Thoughtful Thursdays (encourage reflection on people, events, and moments that have an impact on our lives)

- Fun Fridays (spark creativity or improvisational thinking on the fly)

I offer variety and mystery to make the activity more fun and engaging as well as to stimulate thinking in multiple ways. We could write to some of the same prompts and sparks we offer our students, but I like to use this time to encourage thinking about and responding to issues in our profession that are relevant and timely. We can learn from and about each other as we read different responses to similar sparks. It is important to reiterate that teachers always have the option of keeping their writing private or sharing it with others, and I make this clear before they begin. I created a Daily Digest of volunteered responses to showcase the diversity of our thinking, experiences, and beliefs, which I share in our group. Teachers appreciate seeing the writing of others, which frequently sparks further ideas.

Some participating teachers have their own blogs, classroom newsletters, or personal writing projects; others are looking for an outlet to build a regular writing habit. I truly believe if we create the "write" conditions and make it easier for each of us to be writers, we can kindle a consistent writing habit.

CHALLENGE SPARKS

Organizing sparks into themes helps teachers to build an anticipatory set for their writing while leaving a bit of a mystery for the day's specific challenge. Thematic writing enables us to develop schema around mindfulness, curiosity and wonder, educational issues, or public relations by revisiting those concepts with different entry points each week. If you want to start a writing challenge in your school, think about what topics or themes would most inspire your teachers, and use writing as that spark for self-discovery, community building, and professional support. Here are some ideas to get you started:

Mindful Mondays

- Watch videos on mindfulness and invite teachers to respond.

- Invite teachers to engage in a mindfulness activity or meditation and then write about it.

- Reframe a situation in your day or week that revises the narrative more positively yet honestly. (If perception really is reality, this is a very powerful exercise.)

- Write about a time when you were fully present in the moment (see Figure 8.9).

Write about a time when you were fully present in the moment.

Yesterday I brought Moxie for a walk to try to get some energy out. We went for a two mile hike behind our house. She chased some chipmunks and brought some sticks to play with at home. This was the first time all vacation where I wasn't "plugged in" and it was amazing. I was able to observe my surroundings, the woodpeckers new hole in the tree, the family of chipmunks living under the log, the peepers peeping away. It smelled like springtime for the first time to me. The way the leaves and sticks crunched under my feet while walking, and the scurrying sound of the chipmunks hiding from my obnoxious beagle. In this moment I absorbed everything, in this moment I was present.

Figure 8.9
Mindful Monday quick write

Topical Tuesdays

- Share articles, tweets, or headlines about current hot topics in education (homework, school choice, teacher evaluation, etc.), and invite responses.

- We often forget we speak fluent jargonese. Explain an acronym (RTI, IEP, NBPT, PBIS, etc.) in parent-friendly language.

- Offer sparks that invite greater awareness about our schools, assessments, changes in curriculum and standards, and so on as a public relations activity (see Figure 8.10).

- Instructional and pedagogical approaches can vary from teacher to teacher who uses the same curriculum, so invite teachers to share their best-practice ideas.

Public Relations

We often feel like the public doesn't understand or appreciate what we do.
What do *you* think people don't understand about teaching?

I would like the ability to share what is going on inside my head and heart. The 3am lack of sleep because I am planning my math lesson because half the kids don't understand elapsed time. To be in my heart when I look down at my students' hands and see that they are dirty...still, look and see their toes out the front of their shoes, when they ask for a snack because they are so hungry.

I want them in my head when I am watching my own kids swim in July and I am working through the curriculum. When my Sunday is spent sneaking into school to "get stuff done".

I don't think people understand that I spent a lot of time planning the lesson I just taught and that I will need to use my family time to assess the learning and then plan the next lesson.

I would like people to know that there is never enough time to get it all done, that we love those kids and want them to succeed; that it is not possible to be a counselor, teacher, mother, friend to every kid in our class and do it all well.

Figure 8.10
Topical Tuesday quick write

Wondering Wednesday

- What or who leaves you wondering long after school lets out? Is there a kid you can't stop thinking about? A roadblock you want to overcome? A family that has you worried? Write it out. (See Figure 8.11.)

- If, as Einstein argued, curiosity is more important than knowledge, what is it you are most curious about in life? What do you still want to learn?

- What do you think school looks like through the eyes of your students? Think about a lesson, routine, or conversation in your classroom, and imagine it from a child's perspective. What are they wondering? Thinking?

- What do you imagine school will be like in twenty years? Picture one of your students twenty years from now. What do you imagine him or her doing or being?

That Kid You Can't Stop Thinking About

As teachers we often have at least one student that we can't stop thinking about. We wonder about his/her life. We wonder what they need... We are filled with wonder.
Without naming the student (call him or her X) write about that kid.

      X. The child I stuggle to reach. Quiet, isolated, wouldn't laugh at my silliness. X. Defiant, stubborn; always trying to change what has been asked of him. Hidden sadness. A need to contol something.
      He spoke to me. About pizza. During lunch. It was a breakthrough. I ran with it! I asked him about video games. I asked him what his favorite scary movie is.
      I think about him every morning, night, while driving. How can I continue to make steps into his life?

Figure 8.11
Wondering Wednesday quick write

Thoughtful Thursday

- Consider some themes that invite deeper thought (e.g., overcoming adversity, generosity, inequity, implicit bias). Share an article, video, or quote to stimulate thinking.

- Spread kindness and thoughtfulness by writing about actions from our past or contemplating actions for our future (see Figure 8.12).

- Encourage empathy and understanding for parents, colleagues, administrators, and the public by quick writing about an issue from their perspective.

- Write a thoughtful letter of gratitude or appreciation to someone with the intention of delivering it. Write a letter of advice/encouragement to yourself for the start of next year.

Figure 8.12
**Thoughtful Thursday
quick write**

Thoughtfulness

Reaching out
Spending time
Sending smiles
Choosing kind
Little gestures
Feeling compassion
Helping all
Forgiving wrongs
Surpassing roadblocks
Including strangers
Understanding truths
Embracing love
Creating circumstances
Thinking positive
Working together
Erasing hate

Thoughtfulness

Fun Friday

- I can't encourage the use of poetry enough. Create seed ideas that inspire quick poetry in free verse or micropoem structures (acrostic, haiku, tanka, and so on).

- Listen to a popular song, watch a viral video, or share a meme that sparks a short response in writing (the more positive, the better!).

- Write about an event or the highlights of your day in the style of (and with the skill of) students in the grade you teach. Think about their spelling, word choice, punctuation, and organization, and create a quick write that reflects your appreciation of their writing skills.

- Imagine you were asked to make a toast to a retiring teacher. Imagine that teacher is you. What do you hope to be remembered for? (See Figure 8.13.)

- Create a cartoon with one of the following captions:

  - *My best teaching moment.*

  - *My worst teaching moment.*

  - *From the mouths of babes.*

  - *You had to be there.*

  - *Strange, but true.*

  - *They didn't teach this in college.*

  - *I call a Mulligan.*

Imagine you were asked to make a toast to a retiring teacher.
Imagine that teacher is YOU.
Quick Write a toast that would honor the career of this dedicated professional. What do you hope to be remembered for?

We will miss her positive attitude and smile. She would always be smiling in the halls and welcoming kids as they passed. She made the kids feel loved and cared for.
As a collegue, her smile and attitude brighted my day. She would try to turn tricky situations into learning experiences. That attitude was infectious and spread throughout our school. Even the sour-pusses couldn't help but smile too.

Figure 8.13
Fun Friday quick write

Quick Write Invite
Take three minutes to quick write a response to one of the sparks I've shared. How did you decide which to choose?

Quick Wrap

There are many more approaches for encouraging teacher writing. These are meant to be quick, fun, and achievable steps for building a habit and a writing community. They are invitations for any and all educators to experience the joy and satisfaction of being a writer. I have made it a mission in life to encourage teachers to write and for me to practice what I preach. I think these collaborative and reflective quick writes have been meaningful for our teachers, but you don't have to take my word for it. Here's what a few had to say in a reflective quick write.

> I have found the quick writing to be fun, thought-provoking, and really eye-opening for me. I love writing, and it's honestly not my favorite thing to teach, but [quick writing is] giving me a new perspective on what my students are going through when I give them a prompt. Some of them just sit and can't come up with anything. There were a few sparks with the quick writing that were difficult for me, and it really put me in the shoes of my kiddos. Sometimes they say, "I can't come up with any ideas." I never understood why. Quick writing has given me a look into their world, and now I know why. All in all, it's been a great experience and gotten me thinking about my personal writing again, and opened my eyes with teaching writing!. **—Karen Erdmann, fourth grade**

> Quick writing, a three-minute action to put it all on paper. Paper is a wonderful outlet because it doesn't talk back, judge, or pity. It's something that understands, no matter how honest, raw, and real your day was. Whether it's been a long day, short morning, amazing lesson, or "plan E" afternoon, we all need an outlet, and quick writing has given me that. It brought me back to my pre-service teaching when journaling about your day was required. Why we give that up once we get full-time job is mind-boggling to me. In fact, I believe we need journaling more once we get a job. Quick writing has transformed my school days, and it's all because it's an outlet for me—a place where I can leave it all on paper. It is a safe, reflective way to get everything I need off my chest, to work through problems, see them in a different light, or to celebrate my successes. Three minutes is all it takes to remove the weight of the world from your shoulders and put it all on paper. **—Kaitie King, fourth grade**

I think it is important for teachers to put themselves in the shoes of their students whenever possible so they can get a sense of what students may experience. This can then assist the teacher in making adaptations to their own instruction or expectations because it leads to a better sense of understanding or empathy for the students. Another benefit of having teachers build a writing habit is to help get ideas flowing. Quick writes can be a great way to brainstorm thoughts and get words down on paper that can be further developed at a later point. Writing on the spot is a skill that can be developed and by doing quick writes without the pressure of having them graded or critiqued any further than to express your ideas leads to building that skill without stress or anxiety.
—**Jessica West, math coach**

Quick Write Invite

Do you (or teachers in your school) see yourselves as writers?

What is being done to encourage and support teachers as writers?

References

Barbey, Aron K., et al. 2012. "An Integrative Architecture for General Intelligence and Executive Function Revealed by Lesion Mapping." *Brain* 135 (4): 1154–1164. Retrieved from https://academic.oup.com/brain/article/135/4/1154/358258.

Collaborative for Academic, Social, and Emotional Learning (CASEL). "What Is SEL?" Retrieved from https://casel.org/what-is-sel/.

Covey, Stephen R. 2004. *The 7 Habits of Highly Effective People: Powerful Lessons in Personal Change.* New York: Free Press.

Doward, Jamie. 2017. "Revealed: The More Time That Children Chat on Social Media, the Less Happy They Feel." The *Guardian*. Retrieved from https://www.theguardian.com/society/2017/apr/09/social-networks--children-chat-feel-less-happy-facebook-instagram-whatsapp.

Dredge, Stewart. 2015. "Why YouTube Is the New Children's TV . . . and Why It Matters." The *Guardian*. Retrieved from https://www.theguardian.com/technology/2015/nov/19/youtube-is-the-new-childrens-tv-heres-why-that-matters.

Dweck, Carol S. 2008. *Mind-set: The New Psychology of Success.* New York: Ballantine.

Emmons, Robert. 2010. "Why Gratitude Is Good." *Greater Good Magazine.* Retrieved from https://greatergood.berkeley.edu/article/item/why_gratitude_is_good.

Franken, Robert E. 1994. *Human Motivation.* Pacific Grove, CA: Brooks/Cole.

Graves, Donald H., and Penny Kittle. 2005. *My Quick Writes: For Inside Writing.* Portsmouth, NH: Heinemann.

Greene, Jane, and Anthony M. Grant. 2003. *Solution-Focused Coaching: Managing People in a Complex World.* London: Pearson Education Limited.

Hopkins, Lee Bennett, ed. 2018. *World Make Way: New Poems Inspired by Art from The Metropolitan Museum.* New York: Abrams Books for Young Readers.

Lehrer, Jonah. 2009. "Creation on Command: What We Know." *SeedMagazine.com.* Retrieved from http://seedmagazine.com/content/article/creation_on_command.

Marzano, Robert J., Debra Pickering, and Jane E. Pollock. 2001. *Classroom Instruction That Works: Research-based Strategies for Increasing Student Achievement.* Alexandria, VA: ASCD.

Mosher, Catherine E., and Sharon Danoff-Burg. 2006. "Health Effects of Expressive Letter Writing." *Journal of Social and Clinical Psychology* 25 (10): 1122-1139.

Newkirk, Tom (@Tom_Newkirk). Twitter post, April 14, 2018, 9:09pm. Retrieved from https://twitter.com/Tom_Newkirk/status/985324316442218496.

Ogle, Donna M. 1986. "K-W-L: A Teaching Model That Develops Active Reading of Expository Text." *Reading Teacher* 39: 564-570.

Paivio, Allan. 2006. "Dual Coding Theory and Education." Draft chapter for *Pathways to Literacy Achievement for High-Poverty Children*. Ann Arbor, MI: University of Michigan School of Education. Retrieved from http://www.csuchico.edu/~nschwartz/paivio.pdf.

Pak, Faith A., and Ethan B. Reichsman. 2017. "Beauty and the Brain: The Emerging Field of Neuroaesthetics." *The Harvard Crimson*. Retrieved from https://www.thecrimson.com/article/2017/11/10/neuroaesthetics-cover.

Pak, Sarah S., and Allyson J. Weseley. 2012. "The Effect of Mandatory Reading Logs on Children's Motivation to Read." *Journal of Research in Education* 22 (1): 251-262. Retrieved from https://files.eric.ed.gov/fulltext/EJ1098404.pdf.

Ray, Katie W. 2002. *What You Know by Heart: How to Develop Curriculum for Your Writing Workshop*. Portsmouth, NH: Heinemann.

Remen, Rachel N. 2013, January 11. "Finding New Eyes." *Remembering Your Power to Heal*. Retrieved from www.rachelremen.com/finding-new-eyes.

Rief, Linda. 2003. *100 Quickwrites: Fast and Effective Freewriting Exercises That Build Students' Confidence, Develop Their Fluency, and Bring Out the Writer in Every Student*. Jefferson City, MO: Scholastic Teaching Resources.

Schilling, David R. 2013, April 19. "Knowledge Doubling Every 12 Months, Soon to Be Every 12 Hours." *Industry Tap into News*. Retrieved from http://www.industrytap.com/knowledge-doubling-every-12-months-soon-to-be-every-12-hours/3950.

Toepfer, Steven, and Kathleen Walker. 2009. "Letters of Gratitude: Improving Well-Being Through Expressive Writing." *Journal of Writing Research* 1: 181-198.

Toepfer, Steven, et al. 2012. "Letters of Gratitude: Further Evidence for Author Benefits." *Journal of Happiness Studies* 13: 187-201.

Willis, J. 2011, May 3. "Writing and the Brain: Neuroscience Shows the Pathways to Learning." *National Writing Project*. Retrieved from https://www.nwp.org/cs/public/print/resource/3555.

Index